PLAYING

The Tale of the River Card, Round I

POSSUM

JOHN MARSHALL

iUniverse LLC
Bloomington

PLAYING POSSUM
THE TALE OF THE RIVER CARD, ROUND I

iUniverse books may be ordered through booksellers or by contacting:

iUniverse
1663 Liberty Drive
Bloomington, IN 47403
www.iuniverse.com
1-800-Authors (1-800-288-4677)

ISBN: 978-1-4917-3080-5 (sc)
ISBN: 978-1-4917-3079-9 (e)

Library of Congress Control Number: 2014906895

Printed in the United States of America.

iUniverse rev. date: 04/25/2014

Dedication

This work is dedicated to the three people that I have neglected over the past three years.

I promise to make it up to you as soon as I have finished Round II (and maybe Round III).

- All my Love,

Dad

Contents

Dedication v

Notable Quotes ix

Key Public Testimony and Hearings xi

Preface xv

Acknowledgments xvii

Introduction xix

Chapter 1   Sanctification 1

Chapter 2   Unsung Heroes 6

Chapter 3   The River Card 29

Chapter 4   The Law of the Land 37

Chapter 5   The Jack of Eastland 44

Chapter 6   The Staubach Report 49

Chapter 7   The Austin Meeting 62

Chapter 8   The Opening Hand 78

Chapter 9   The Missed Deal 93

Chapter 10   Think Long, Think Wrong 105

Chapter 11   The Hail Mary 128

Intermission 139

Notable Quotes

"The governor has supported this since day one. He wants the people at PK to be able to own their properties if they wish."
—Lewis Simmons Chief of Staff to Texas State Senator Craig Estes

"Representatives from Perry's office—Ken Anderson, Phil Wilson, and Cody Shorter—were actively involved in the process all day Tuesday."
—Monte Land, Possum Kingdom Lake Association Chairman

"It's not whether you're going to be raped or not; it's just at what extreme are you going to."
—P. J. Ellison, Brazos River Authority Board Director

"They are asking us to gut a state agency and my hand won't be on that knife."
—Wade Gear, Brazos River Authority Board Director

"The next state park for sale, I want it!"
—Billy Wayne Moore, Brazos River Authority Board Director

"You're smiling too much, Senator; you're giving yourself away."
—Lt. Governor David Dewhurst (on the floor of the Texas Senate to State Senator Estes)

"Divestiture is going to happen."

—Lewis Simmons, Chief of Staff to Texas State Senator Craig Estes

"The legislature is a very powerful force and the BRA has most likely realized that fact."

—Joe Shannon, Tarrant County District Attorney

Key Public Testimony and Hearings

See www.playingpossum.org for a user-friendly presentation of the audio and video records of the official proceedings related to Senate Bill 1326, House Bill 3031, and this transaction.

2006. April 11: The Brazos River Authority

The Staubach Report is presented to the Board of the Brazos River Authority.

Development and Execution of a Comprehensive Property Management Strategy for Possum Kingdom Lake (Phase III Report); Adjourn

http://www.brazos.org/board_audio/04112006_PK-AM4.mp3

2006. May 22: The Brazos River Authority

The Board of the Brazos River Authority meets to vote on the Staubach Report.

Special Board Meeting

Agenda Item 10 (Part 1): Property Management Strategy for Possum Kingdom Lake

http://www.brazos.org/board_audio/05222006_Special_PK_BRD8.mp3

Agenda Items 11–14: Executive Session; Reconvene in Open Session; Action on Items Discussed in Executive Session

http://www.brazos.org/board_audio/05222006_Special_PK_BRD9.mp3

2007. March 26: The Brazos River Authority

The Board of the Brazos River Authority meets to discuss the first attempt at forced divestiture.

Special Board Meeting #2

Agenda Items 5–6: Divestiture Bills SB1326 & HB2923; Adjourn

http://www.brazos.org/board_audio/03262007_1SPL2.mp3

2007. April 17: The Senate Natural Resources Committee

State Senator Craig Estes presents Senate Bill 3126 and declares it a "local" matter.

rtsp://realvideoe.senate.state.tx.us:554/archives/2007/APR/041707.c580.rm.

2007. April 23: The Senate Natural Resources Committee

State Senator Kip Averitt allows Senate Bill 1326 to move forward to a Senate vote.

rtsp://realvideoe.senate.state.tx.us:554/archives/2007/APR/042307.c580.rm.

2007. April 27: The Brazos River Authority

The Board of the Brazos River Authority meets to discuss the handshake deal between State Senator Estes and State Senator Averitt. This was the day that things started to get ugly.

Emergency Board Meeting

Agenda Items 5–6: Response to Proposed Language for Committee Substitute to Senate Bill 1326 Pursuant to Legislative Inquiries; Adjourn

http://www.brazos.org/board_audio/04272007_EME2.mp3

2007. May 4: The Texas Senate

State Senator Craig Estes presents his handshake deal to the full body of the Texas Senate.

http://www.senate.state.tx.us/avarchive/ramav.php?ram=00003415.

2007. May 16: The House Natural Resources Committee

State Representative Jim Keffer leads Senate Bill 1326 into the mouth of hell.

rtsp://realvideoe.house.state.tx.us:554/archives/cmte80r/70516a30.rm.

2007. May 22: The Texas House of Representatives

State Representative Dan Branch attempts to resurrect Senate Bill 1326.

rtsp://realvideoe.house.state.tx.us:554/archives/hc80/052207a.rm.

2007. May 25: The Texas House of Representatives

The Texas Speaker of the House, Tom Craddick, self-destructs.

http://www.house.state.tx.us/fx/av/chamber80/052507a.ram.

2007. May 27: The Texas Senate

State Senators Chris Harris and Craig Estes give State Senator Kip Averitt a public ass-chewing like none other. Their respective do-better letters are reduced to the Senate journal.

rtsp://realvideoe.senate.state.tx.us:554/archives/2007/MAY/052707.session.rm.

Preface

In the fall of 2009, an unusually complex land deal involving the state of Texas was generating an unusual amount of buzz in the bars that I patronize around downtown Dallas.

Early on, it occurred to me that this deal might be juiced. One of the most obvious signs was the fact that the man who was fronting the transaction had earned himself a nickname, the River Card. No one ever used his real name when they were pondering the potential return of an investment in his deal.

By the time that I got a look at the River Card's deal it was way too late. The roster of investors was frozen after the first forty-eight hours, which was a clear indication that I had missed out on something special. It was not too long afterward when the lucky few started bragging about how much money they had made and how fast they had made it.

This was the kind of sure thing that only comes along ever so often. To say the least, missing out on the River Card's deal was a wake-up call for me. Not wanting to make the same mistake twice, I resolved myself to spend more time drinking in the bars around downtown Dallas. I also promised myself that I would research the origins of this deal to ensure that I did not miss out on any subsequent or similar transactions.

The more I studied the River Card's deal, the more I realized how much money I had missed out on. I also came to the conclusion that

I owed it to the younger investors in my crowd to reduce this deal to writing so that they could learn from my mistakes. This was my chance to give back to the investment community that has given so much to me.

The pages that follow represent my attempt to do just that.

Acknowledgments

To the small group of journalists and investigative reporters who have suffered through my endless series of insufferable questions regarding everything from grammar to libel—many thanks to you all. As soon as this topic gets handed off to the pros, the readers will know who you are. And, at that point, you guys and gals can have at it. I cannot wait to watch you all go to work.

To that young woman who shared a hospital waiting room with me and my family last summer, I am deeply and genuinely sorry for your loss. My father came through his surgery *just fine,* as the doctors put it, while yours did not.

Watching you and your two daughters and the rest of your family hold hands was nothing short of heartwarming. Watching you and those girls have to visit with that priest was nothing short of heartbreaking. Your grace and dignity in that moment was the catalyst that made me decide to finish this. Godspeed, and best of luck in your endeavors.

Introduction

If you can keep your head when all about you are losing
theirs ...

Rudyard Kipling penned those words in 1895 and went on to advocate
trust, truth, virtue, and betting it all on the river card.[1]

While his words were thoughtful, they were not necessarily actionable,
as he neglected to specify when to go all-in. This is especially true if you
define action as separating a man from his money or from his real estate.
Although Rudyard lived in the United States for four years, there is no
evidence that he ever stepped foot in the state of Texas, and he probably
never once played a hand of Texas Hold'em. If he had, he might have
learned what defines the true measure of a man.

In January 2009, it seemed that everyone was losing their head and
then some. Everyone that is, except for the River Card. He never blinked.

Those who regulate, marshal, and otherwise steer the American
economic system were collectively convinced in January 2009 that we
were all staring into the abyss. The S&P 500 had just lost ten years' worth
of value and the Great Recession was in full swing. Names like Bear
Stearns and Lehman Brothers had been reduced to entries in the history
books, and the US Treasury Department was rebranding itself on a daily
basis. Annual bonuses for bankers and brokers were in question, and

---

1   Well, more or less.

there was even talk that freshly minted Harvard MBAs might not find jobs upon graduation. Fortune 500 CEOs were flying commercial for the sake of public relations, and their CFOs were packing their dry powder into storage kegs and stashing them away accordingly. The US financial markets were paralyzed.

Since the executives on Wall Street are the only ones who actually know what an abyss looks like, the rest of us were required to look through their prism and gasp on cue. Expecting an abyss to be something filled with brimstone or maybe some flying snow monkeys, 90 percent of us were eventually relieved to learn that an abyss is simply a basket of pink slips that get handed out to the other 10 percent of the workforce. For the remaining 90 percent of us who kept our jobs, an abyss turned out to be something that actually created lower prices for food, cars, gasoline, electronic devices, stocks, lake houses and, most important, the ground beneath those lake houses.

In Washington, DC, change was in the air. Who knows whether the American voters looked into the abyss and recoiled or simply considered the next option offered by the Republican Party to be abysmal?[2] For the first time in twenty years, a man who did not hail from Texas or Arkansas was about to be installed as the president of the United States. Moreover, the president-elect appeared to be the fulfillment of Martin Luther King's dream and he captured the attention of every vein of the media. As a result, no one gave a possum's ass about local issues, such as the sale of surplus real estate in Palo Pinto County, Texas.

In Austin, Texas, January 2009 was noteworthy for decidedly different reasons.

Four years earlier, US Senator Kay Bailey Hutchison from Texas had mounted and then abandoned a challenge against incumbent Texas governor Rick Perry. On January 14, 2009, Todd J. Gillman of the *Dallas Morning News* reported that Senator Hutchison would be mounting a second challenge in 2010.[3] Perry and Hutchison were both tenured leaders in the Texas Republican Party, and the party faithful would be forced to choose sides.

---

2   John McCain and Sarah Palin?

3   Todd J. Gillman, "Hutchinson Mounts Challenge," *Dallas Morning News,* January 14, 2009.

At the outset, Kay Bailey Hutchinson enjoyed a twenty-five-point lead in the polls, and major newspapers across the state were endorsing her candidacy. Rick Perry had never lost an election at any level, and losing to Hutchinson would surely doom his 2012 presidential bid before it even got started. In the face of this challenge, Perry could not have enough friends with money in their pockets and influence at their disposal. Now was the time for Perry to put his reputation as a governor who "transparently rewards friends and punishes enemies" to good use.[4] The contest for the governor's mansion was shaping up to be a repeat of Clayton Williams vs. Ann Richards.[5]

Simultaneously, one of the largest battles in the history of the Texas legislature was reaching its climax. The Speaker of the House, a man by the name of Tom Craddick from Midland, had managed to alienate the entire House of Representatives. The power struggle that followed in both parties became known as the "Anyone but Craddick" sweepstakes. The number of ambitious representatives seeking the Speaker's gavel was approaching double digits and so too were the horse-trading opportunities that arose from the process.

Tom Craddick began his political career at the age of twenty-five when he ran for the Texas House of Representatives as a Republican. By his own admission, most people thought him foolish as Texas was a one-party state run by the Democrats. Coattails are a powerful thing in politics, however, and the voters of Midland elected Craddick, along with Richard M. Nixon, in 1968. Tom Craddick became one of only nine Republicans in the 150-seat House of Representatives.

In the wake of the Sharpstown stock-fraud scandal, he quickly rose to prominence as a reformer. On January 11, 2003, after thirty-four years in the House, Craddick became the first Republican Speaker in more than 130 years. He held the presiding officer's position for six years.

---

4   "Rick Perry is 2010 Texan of the Year," Editorial, *Dallas Morning News*, December 26, 2010.

5   During his gubernatorial campaign against Ann Richards in 1990, Williams publicly made a joke likening rape to bad weather, having quipped, "If it's inevitable, just relax and enjoy it." His 20 percentage-point lead evaporated and Ann Richards became governor of Texas.

Unfortunately, exercising power became Speaker Craddick's drug of choice. He established a reputation as a tyrant, and a mutiny broke out on the floor of the House on Friday, May 25, 2007.[6] A fellow Republican, Representative Fred Hill, attempted to raise a question of privilege to remove Craddick from office. Craddick refused to allow the question. When Representative Hill requested a vote, the Speaker replied, "The Speaker's power of recognition on any matter cannot be appealed." Those turned out to be Tom's famous last words as Speaker of the House. At the beginning of the next legislative session in January 2009, a full-blown power grab was under way.

A new Speaker of the House would mean new committee chairs and new committee members. This was the flop that the River Card needed, and it married up perfectly with the suited jack-queen that he was holding in the pocket. The River Card was staring at a royal flush. The only thing left to do was play possum, get the pot up, and take everyone else out.

The River Card knew that it was time to go all-in.

The Tale of the River Card is best told backwards. The beginning of the ending occurred on April 8, 2009, when the River Card offered $50 million to buy roughly 1,200 acres of surplus real estate from the state of Texas. Those in the know on this deal valued that same property at roughly $1 billion.

As the story goes, the ensuing transaction represented a case study in collaborative commerce, where a collection of strategic partners worked in unison to achieve a mutually beneficial outcome. If everyone got what they wanted, then *The Tale of the River Card* must be without a victim. In the absence of a victim, there can be no crime per se and thus no motives that need to be examined. In the absence of a crime, there is simply no story worth telling outside of academia.

Unfortunately, there are no business schools in Palo Pinto County, Texas, to speak of, and so far both Wharton and Harvard have neglected to give this transaction its due. Thus, the task falls to a guy whose capacity for being politically correct is limited to saying "See, I told you so."

---

6   Tom Craddick, "House Session," *Texas House of Representatives Broadcast Archives*, May 25, 2007, accessed November 18, 2010. http://www.house.state.tx.us/fx/av/chamber80/052507a.ram.

The reason that the book you are holding is covered by a picturesque aerial photo of a lake in Texas, the most notable attribute of which in 1941 was an overabundance of possums, is to ensure that you can recoup your investment by decorating your coffee table.

I have learned over the years that there are usually two sides to every story. This is true whether you are talking about an ugly divorce or the sale of surplus real estate in Palo Pinto County. As the other side of the story goes, the taxpayers of Texas got screwed like a bunch of tied-up goats.[7]

Welcome to the great state of Texas, where we are "Wide Open for Business."[8]

---

7   That, of course, is a reference to the scene in *Jurassic Park* (Amblin Entertainment, 1993) where they tied that poor little goat to a post and fed him to T. Rex. What were you thinking it meant?

8   Governor Rick Perry's motto is "Wide Open for Business." You have to admit that it is better than "Oops."

Chapter 1

SANCTIFICATION

On May 27, 2009, House Bill 3031 was signed by Texas governor Rick Perry, authorizing the Brazos River Authority to sell a few hundred acres of surplus real estate in the immediate vicinity of Possum Kingdom Lake. The bill enjoyed unanimous consent in both the House and the Senate. Throughout the entire process, not one single vote was cast in opposition.

House Bill 3031 was authored by State Representative James L. (Jim) Keffer of House District 60. His fifty-two-page opus was filed on March 10, 2009, and then referred to the House Natural Resources Committee. On April 7, Representative Keffer appeared before this committee to explain his bill, which carried the following caption:

> **"Relating to the sale by the Brazos River Authority of certain residential and commercial leased lots and other real property in the immediate vicinity of Possum Kingdom Lake."**

During his remarks, Representative Keffer stated that HB 3031 was the product of six years of hard work and that "even today, there is no easy explanation of this bill." At the end of his presentation he declared, "I'm proud to present you an agreed-to bill." There were no questions from the

1

committee members present and no opposing testimony offered. The entire hearing lasted only nine minutes and thirty-five seconds.[9]

In the absence of a dissenting voice, the bill was referred to the Local and Consent Calendar Committee.[10] On April 28, HB 3031 and ninety-one other uncontested bills were laid on the House floor and voted on, en masse. The vote was recorded as 149 yeas, 0 nays, and 1 present, not voting. The unanimously approved bill was sent to the Senate and routed to the Agriculture and Rural Affairs Committee. This would be the final hand that the River Card would need to take down the pot, and State Senator Craig Estes would be dealing the cards.

On May 11, 2009, House Bill 3031 endured a second and final public hearing. With only three of the five committee members present, Senator Estes laid out HB 3031 and explained that it was an "agreed-to" matter and thus could be considered "enabling legislation." Again, there was no opposing testimony offered, and only one member of the committee would pose a question. During testimony, State Senator Mike Jackson asked how the real estate would be appraised. He then turned to Senator Estes and asked whether or not the property would be sold for fair market value. While Estes' reply was inaudible on the video archive, his response seemed to satisfy Senator Jackson.

When State Senator Glenn Hegar arrived to establish a quorum, Senator Estes moved that the bill be reported favorably, and the motion carried unanimously. The chair of the committee then moved that the bill be placed on the Local and Uncontested Calendar and without objection, it was so ordered.

Four days later, the bill was laid on the floor of the Texas senate where it was unanimously approved by thirty senators. Four days after that, it was signed in both the House and the Senate and sent to the governor. On May 27, it received Governor Rick Perry's signature and became

---

9   Rep. Jim Keffer, "House Natural Resources Committee," *Texas House of Representatives Broadcast Archives*, April 7, 2009, accessed November 19, 2010. http://www.house.state.tx.us/video-audio/committee-broadcasts/committee-archives/player/?session=81&committee=390&ram=90407b24.

10   This means that it was worthy of being rubber-stamped by the entire House of Representatives without further debate or deliberation.

effective immediately. Obviously, House Bill 3031 represented the will of the people.

The odd thing about House Bill 3031 is that the property in question had already been sold to the River Card for pennies on the dollar. While the Texas legislature was busy considering the will of the people, the Brazos River Authority had been busy selling the land. On January 8, 2009, the BRA put the property up for sale by posting a "request for bids" on their website. The deadline to submit a bid was April 8, which created a ninety-day window. Given that most real estate investors were busy staring into the abyss, the response was somewhat underwhelming. Only two bids were received, and as lady luck would have it, The River Card was the high bid.

There were other curious things about House Bill 3031, starting with the text of the bill's caption:

"Relating to the sale by the Brazos River Authority of certain residential and commercial leased lots and other real property in the immediate vicinity of Possum Kingdom Lake."

As it turns out, the term "immediate vicinity" actually meant "lakefront," and the term "leased lots" referred to the dirt beneath the luxury homes that had been built along the shoreline. Even stranger was the fact that HB 3031 mandated that any party that purchased the property that had already been sold would then turn around and resell the individual lots at a fixed price to the individuals who had built those luxury homes. (Is anyone confused yet?) With the term "toxic assets" dominating the business news at the time, the BRA's public offering proved more confusing than compelling.

Another odd thing about House Bill 3031 is the fact that similar legislation, Senate Bill 1326, had met a humiliating defeat twenty-four months earlier. In 2007, the board and staff of the Brazos River Authority testified passionately against the measure. Senator Kip Averitt, who was also the chairman of the Senate Natural Resources Committee, voted to refer Senate Bill 1326 to the floor of the Senate and then voted against the bill when it got there. Evidently, the will of the people is as fluid as the Brazos River itself.

Before you continue, you will need a good understanding of the concept of fair market value. Fair market value is an estimate of the market value of a piece of property, based on what a knowledgeable, willing, and unpressured buyer would probably pay to a knowledgeable, willing, and unpressured seller in the real estate market. Make no mistake about this: the River Card was the most knowledgeable guy in the room, more than willing to make a fortune, and under no pressure to do so. Conversely, the Brazos River Authority did not have a clue on the day that they voted to sell the property, did not want to participate in "welfare for the wealthy" prior to the transaction, and had absolutely no say-so in the matter.

You will also need a solid understanding of what a "fee simple estate" is. Simply put, a fee simple estate is a clear title to a piece of property. There are no claims or encumbrances that would grant anyone else access to or use of the property. It is yours to do with as you see fit.

The worst thing by far about HB 3031 is that when Senator Mike Jackson was convinced that the $1 billion worth of property would be sold for fair market value, Senator Estes was far less than forthcoming. Nowhere within the fifty-two pages of HB 3031 is there any reference to fair market value. Instead, the bill mandated that the property be resold to the individuals who had built their weekend homes along the shoreline for 65 percent of their 2008 property tax valuations.

At least, that was the case on the day that the bill was filed. On April 9, the day after the River Card submitted his winning bid to buy the property, HB 3031 was amended and the fixed price at which the River Card was required to resell the property changed to 90 percent of the 2008 property tax valuations.

Based on the tax rolls, that amendment changed the total resell price of the collective lots from $65 million to $90 million and provided the River Card with an overnight windfall of $25 million. Based on his bid of $50 million, the amendment put his total take at $40 million during one of the worst financial meltdowns in the history of the United States. This would all seem extremely fortuitous were it not for the fact that the River Card was intimately involved in the drafting and crafting of House Bill 3031.

In reality, House Bill 3031 was a damn dirty piece of legislation that was designed to legitimize a property-laundering scheme that was already in motion, albeit with a significant enhancement. The true purpose of the bill was simple. There were laws on the books that were intended to prevent a transaction of this nature from happening, and HB 3031 castrated those laws.

To make a long story short, this deal was driven by wealthy individuals who had secured the services of a state representative from Eastland, a state senator from Wichita Falls, the Texas attorney general, the lieutenant governor who presided over the Senate, and the governor of the state of Texas. The undisputed legislation transferred roughly $1 billion worth of prime Texas real estate to a relatively small group of extremely wealthy people for pennies on the dollar. Along the way, the resulting laundering process put over $40 million in the River Card's pocket.

Nonetheless, you cannot argue with the will of the people. It does seem fair to ask, however, "Exactly, who the hell are these people?"

Let's go ask the River Card.

Chapter 2

UNSUNG HEROES

Texans are nothing if not polite. As a general rule, they know how to say thank-you.

Shortly after the Brazos River Authority voted to accept the River Card's bid for the property, he posted the following expression of gratitude on his website.[11] Perhaps this will offer a hint as to whose will HB 3031 was intended to satisfy.

Patterson PK Land Partnership Ltd.

Unsung Heroes

Recently I (Mike Patterson) have been receiving too much of the credit (and some of the cussing) for fielding a successful bid that will let 1,583 PK BRA lessees finally buy their (our) land at 2008 land only assessed values. But like the little duck that seems to glide effortlessly across the pond, just out of site [sic] there was always a lot of furious paddling going on by many others. I am

---

11   Mike Patterson, "Unsung Heroes," *PK Land Partnership*, Patterson Equity Partners, n.d., accessed February 1, 2010. (This web page has since been removed, but through the magic of Google, the text has been preserved and archived for the inevitable lawsuit. Formatting has been added for readability.)

sure I will miss many, but I want to go ahead and recognize the following individuals for their help and support:

–   Lance Byrd—He was my inspiration to get involved. I watched from the sidelines in 2007 as he, with the help of a few, almost pushed divestiture to the goal line in the 80th legislative session. His leadership and determination inspired me to get involved.

–   Jay Propes—Jay was the lobbyist (The Graydon Group) in Austin that helped navigate me through the political landmines. I hooked on to Jay's wagon and just held on. Initially working for free until I could afford to hire him and after I hired him still significantly underpaid, Jay deserves much of the credit. I have promised him, if ever given the opportunity, I will name something after him. That scares him a little bit.

–   Senator Estes—Senate Sponsor of HB 3031. Numero Uno!!! He makes me want to move to PK just so I can vote for him.

–   Lewis Simmons (Senator Estes' Chief of Staff)—invisible to most, but did the heavy lifting to keep all doors open and the ball always moving forward.

–   Senator Kip Averitt—Don't let anybody ever tell you he was not our friend in this effort.

–   Representatives Jim Keffer, Paula Pierson and Jim Jackson—We should always be forever thankful for their authorship and carrying of HB 3031.

–   BRA

    Phil Ford—Nothing but a gentleman. Pure professional.

    Matt Phillips—I think I wore him out, but he never complained. I think he sleeps with his BlackBerry by his side. He was most helpful.

–   Mark Engebretson with the *Lake Country Sun*. Mark has been tireless and has kept up the necessary coverage to keep all of us adequately informed.

–   Rebecca Lucas—Always unwavering support.

–   Marsha Bettis—Always unwavering support.

–   Friends—Friends in need are friends indeed!!! Thank you guys for hanging with me!

    Eric Nelson

    Chris Ringel

    Jim Maibach

    Greg McCarthy

    Bennett Carter

– Banks and Bankers: These guys helped fund me the 2.5 million earnest money to get and keep the BRA on contract.

> First National Bank of Graham—Bob Coleman, Del Lee and Glenn McGee
>
> Affiliated Bank—Garry Graham and Bennett Carter
>
> Southwest Securities, FSB—John Holt and Del Waller

– The "Wichita Falls" support group. Led by Earl Denny and Tommy McCullough (Tommy is a lessee and President of Fidelity Bank in Wichita Falls). You got the ball rolling for us.

– Attorneys

> George Gault—a lawyer's lawyer. If I stay out of trouble on this deal, it will be because of George's wise and learned counsel.

– PKLA—cautious, careful and always having the best of intentions. We can never thank them enough! Thanks Carolyn and Monte for all you both continue to do for us all!!!

> Many thanks to all the above.
>
> Mike

You would have to be a really old man who has been around here for a really long time for any of these names, or banks, or organizations to mean anything to you. You would also have to be a financial genius to understand how someone could purchase $1 billion worth of real estate for $50 million when he could not even afford to pay his lobbyist or put up his own earnest money.

And that's where yours truly comes in.

If you have the patience to follow this story, I will explain who the "unsung heroes" are and why they matter. If I can keep your attention long enough, I will also explain who the real players were and why this matter went as far as it did.

If you have ever been forced to apply the Harvard Case Study methodology to a business scenario, then you know that step one is to perform a cursory analysis of the key stakeholders. Cognitive dissonance is the enemy of any corporate strategy, and it is important to understand both the personal and professional motives of those involved.

So, in deference to Michael Porter, the father of the Harvard Case Study, rather than Michael Patterson, the "little duck gliding effortlessly across the pond," let's segment these heroes into groups of players with common interests, starting with the easiest to understand.

The Politicians and the Bureaucrats

It is convenient to say that the only thing politicians in Texas want is to get reelected, but this is entirely unfair. Once they reach their second term, they also desperately want to move up the food chain. After that, they want to solidify and monetize their seniority and their tenure.

For a politician with higher aspirations, the divestiture of $1 billion worth of prime Texas real estate to a collection of doctors, lawyers, and bankers for pennies on the dollar was an opportunity that does not come along every day. The largesse was so extreme that Wade Gear, the secretary of the board of the Brazos River Authority, declared during an emergency meeting held on April 27, 2007:

> "They are asking us to gut a state agency and my hand won't be on that knife."

It wasn't. Governor Rick Perry replaced Director Wade Gear during the ninety-day sealed bid process.

Perhaps more valuable than the largesse involved was the profile of the recipients of the welfare. We are talking about weekend homes here, meaning that the owners hailed from somewhere else. The resulting mailing list of thankful constituents spanned North Texas and beyond. There were 1,583 of them. If you wanted to run for a statewide office or perhaps wrap one of your hands around the Speaker's gavel, then these folks represented a potential war chest like none other.

House Bill 3031 was sponsored by Senator Craig Estes from Wichita Falls, and he was relentless in his pursuit of its passage. Senator Estes was also two years wiser. In the previous legislative session of 2007, he had led the charge on divestiture by both authoring and sponsoring Senate Bill 1326. During that effort, he had managed to achieve a handshake deal with Senator Kip Averitt, wherein they agreed that the Brazos River

Authority would only be asked to leave roughly $20 million on the table when they sold the property to the weekenders. Their deal ran into a snag when one of the Brazos River Authority's few female board directors, Pamela Ellison, stated on the record, and on the verge of tears,

It's not whether you're going to be raped or not, it's just at what extreme are you going to.[12]

Thanks to another politician from Midland by the name of Clayton Williams, Republicans in Texas are a bit touchy when the term "rape" is used during official proceedings. It was immediately obvious to the policy makers that they had failed to do a thorough job of socializing their plan with the people who would eventually be asked to give it their blessing. They had also failed to properly stack the deck. When the same female board director added that she had "a real problem with the Governor and Lt. Governor telling board members not to attend meetings and hearings," the handshake deal was doomed. When SB 1326 reached the floor of the Senate, Senator Averitt voted nay.

On his second attempt at divestiture during the 2009 legislative session, Senator Estes employed the services of a few surrogates. House Bill 3031 was authored by Representative Jim Keffer and was coauthored by Representatives Paula Pierson[13] of Arlington and Jim Jackson of Carrolton. We'll examine Keffer in detail downstream, but make a quick note here that Pierson and Jackson represent districts that are fifty miles removed from the Brazos River. The only thing about the Brazos that affected their constituents was the price of the dirt sitting under their weekend homes on Possum Kingdom Lake.

Texas is a rather large place and enjoys the public service of 150 state representatives. Its longest river, the Brazos, runs through the center of the state for 840 miles and borders or crosses over forty counties. If you are thinking that Senator Estes surely could have found at least one member

---

12   Pamela Ellison, "Emergency Board Meeting—Agenda Items 5–6," Brazos River Authority Board of Directors Audio Meetings Minutes, 37:23, April 27, 2007, accessed November 28, 2010. http://www.brazos.org/board_audio/04272007_EME2.mp3.

13   Paula Pierson defeated Toby Goodman in 2006 in the wake of his "rent-to-own" ethics investigation.

of the House with a district bordering the Brazos River to coauthor his "agreed-to" bill, then you simply don't understand how the poker game of politics works in Texas. You don't waste good pork on just anyone.

Being asked to coauthor HB 3031 was an offer that Democrat Paula Pierson could not afford to refuse. She had defeated Toby Goodman three years earlier in the wake of his ethics investigation, and the Arlington district that she won was considered a Republican stronghold. To say the least, she needed to win the affinity of the Republican powerbrokers in Dallas, Ft. Worth, Arlington, and Austin. Moreover, the fact that she was one of very few Democrats representing a district in Tarrant County made her a fund-raising machine. During the 2010 election cycle, she came just shy of joining the $1 million club in donations, including the $5,000 that the River Card pitched in on June 30, 2009—three days after he signed his contract to purchase the entire inhabited shoreline of Possum Kingdom Lake.

By contrast, Senator Kip Averitt knew that the Possum Kingdom divestiture deal was an unflattering case study waiting to be written. At every opportunity, Averitt publicly washed his hands of the responsibility. Nonetheless, "Don't let anybody ever tell you he was not our friend in this effort." Senator Averitt would aid the River Card's cause in due course and would be rewarded handsomely for it.

As for the River Card's two bureaucratic heroes, Phil Ford and Matt Phillips, of the Brazos River Authority, simply wanted to keep their paychecks. (This kind of reminds me of the rest of us during the financial meltdown.)

During an annual meeting of the Possum Kingdom Lake Association in 2007, Senator Estes' chief of staff, Lewis Simmons, stated that "divestiture was 'going to happen' and that it is hoped that the BRA will take a more proactive posture in arranging the divesture." He further stated "that with the assistance of Governor Perry and Lieutenant Governor Dewhurst, hopes are high that a solution can be worked out before the next session."[14] When this sentiment reached the hired help at the BRA, they got on board accordingly.

---

14 "Annual Membership Meeting Summary," *Possum Kingdom Lake Association*, June 23, 2007, accessed December 12, 2010. http://www.pklakeassn.org/June%2023%20 Annual%20Meeting.htm.

Before you judge them too harshly, remember that in late 2008 and early 2009, we were all staring into the abyss, and the market for unemployed water board executives was fairly soft. Beyond that point, Phil Ford received a $75,000 bonus in July 2007; an $85,000 bonus in 2008, 2009, 2010, 2011, and 2012; and a 20 percent raise in 2013, which brought his total compensation package to roughly $300,000. That's good work during a recession, if you can find it.

The Bankers

It is no secret that bankers are in the business of loaning people a certain sum of money with the expectation of being repaid a larger sum of money at a later date. The question then becomes this: Why would dozens of intelligent bankers lend tens of millions of dollars to a man who couldn't afford the earnest money for a $50 million deal and couldn't afford to pay his lobbyist? The answer is simple: the game was rigged, and they wanted in on the action.

Any bank that loaned the River Card a portion of the $50 million that he needed to purchase the property was granted "preferred lender" status. That was a term invented by the River Card. Any homeowner who, in turn, purchased the land under his or her home from the River Card and financed the transaction through a preferred lender was granted a 15 percent discount off the price tag.

Only a fool would pass on this deal, and if you are going to finance your dirt, you might as well refinance your dwelling and roll it all into one note. During his recruitment process for the preferred lenders, the River Card himself valued this pool of premium mortgage paper at over $1 billion. In the final analysis, we will see that this cartel of bankers actually made more money off this transaction than the River Card and the state of Texas put together. Suffice it to say that the River Card's banking cartel was a group of enthusiastic participants.

Topping this list of enthusiastic participants was the First National Bank in Graham, which served as the lead lender and was managed by Mr. Bob Coleman, Mr. Del Lee, and Mr. Glenn McGee. The First National Bank in Graham is a modest institution located on Elm Street that enjoyed a total asset base of $220 million at the end of 2008. Since the River Card needed a bankroll equating to roughly one-fourth of its total size, this deal was a bit beyond their legal lending limit. Mr. Coleman and his team were in need of some partners.

One bank that stepped up to the challenge was First Financial Bank. First Financial is a considerably larger institution that described itself to potential Possum Kingdom customers on the River Card's website in the following fashion:

> First Financial Bankshares, Inc. is a family of community banks with 48 locations, more than 67 ATMs and six Trust offices across Texas. At First Financial, "customer service first" isn't just a philosophy, it's the way we do business with each and every bank customer. As a result, in its first-quarter 2009 issue, Bank Directors Magazine selected First Financial Bankshares, Inc. as the Best Bank in TEXAS AND the # 2 bank in the nation in the $3 billion plus publicly traded category. Generations of families, professionals, and business owners in Texas have relied on First Financial for the best in banking and wealth management services for more than a century.[15]

At fifteen times the size of the little bank in Graham, First Financial brought true lending power to the equation. More importantly, they also brought some political clout and some "wise and learned counsel" to the table. Serving on the board of directors of First Financial Bank, Eastland, was none other than State Representative James L. (Jim) Keffer, the official author of HB 3031. Serving on the board of directors of First Financial Bank, Mineral Wells, was the River Card's lawyer, Mr. George S. Gault.

Perhaps the most intriguing preferred lender is Affiliated Bank of Arlington. The chairman and CEO of Affiliated Bank is a gentleman by the name of Gary Graham, who is ably assisted by Executive Vice President Bennett Carter. Serving as an advisory director for Affiliated is Mr. Eric Nelson.

Mr. Graham, Mr. Carter, and Mr. Nelson actually enjoyed double-preferred status, as they were also given an equity reservation of $500,000 each in the River Card's private placement that was used to finance the

---

15   Mike Patterson, "First Financial Bank," *PK Land Partnership*, Patterson Equity Partners, n.d., accessed November 20, 2013. http://www.pklandpartnership.com/FirstFinancial. aspx.

equity tranche of this transaction. Those are some of your "friends in need."

Bringing up the rear of the preferred lenders is Fidelity Bank of Wichita Falls, led by President Tommy McCullough, who "got the ball rolling for us." To be fair, it was Dennis Cannedy, who serves on the board of directors of Fidelity Bank, who got the ball rolling. At the time, Dennis Cannedy was also the campaign treasurer for State Senator Craig Estes.

During his initial conference call with his preferred lenders, held on November 24, 2009, the River Card explained that Southwest Securities, FSB, had asked to be excused from his deal, as it had recently exited the mortgage loan market.[16] While this sounds like a reasonable explanation, the truth of the matter is that the CEO of Southwest Securities, FSB, considered the River Card's deal to be toxic. CEO John Holt's reasoning was twofold.

The first problem that Holt had with this deal was the raw land. In the original vote to issue a request for bids, the Brazos River Authority had intended to sell the entirety of its real estate holdings, including the uninhabited land. Being one of those executives who actually knew what an abyss looks like, John Holt also knew that his bank examiners would consider any such loan to be a toxic asset.

Holt also had a major problem with the fact that the River Card was serving on the board of his bank at the time, along with one of his "friends in need," Mr. Jim Maibach. When Holt informed the River Card that Southwest Securities was backing out of his deal, the latter became hotter than a half-fornicated fox in a forest fire.

As our case study progresses, other bankers will enter the picture. Of note among these is Mr. Peter Bennis, who is the president and chief executive officer for Pinnacle Bank, one of the River Card's preferred lenders. Mr. Bennis was also a board director for the Brazos River Authority.

Another banker that will enter the story is Ms. Mary Ward, the president of Government Affairs for Southwest Securities, FSB. You guessed it, Ms. Ward was also a board director of the Brazos River Authority. And while

---

16 Mike Patterson, "Initial Preferred Lender Conference Call," *PK Land Partnership*, Patterson Equity Partners, November 24, 2009, accessed November 20, 2013. www. pklandpartnership.com/downloads/Inital%20Preferred%20Lender%20Confrence%20 Call%2011-24-09.mp3.

she officially reported to John Holt at the time, she acted as though she reported to the River Card.

The Lawyers and the Lobbyists

Isn't it interesting that a lawyer would need a lawyer? The firm of Gault & Gault specializes in civil law, family law, oil and gas law, real estate law, municipal law, and probate law. As this story develops, it will be interesting to see how many of these services the River Card will require. The firm of Gault & Gault was also one of only two approved title attorneys for the River Card's deal.

The relationship between the River Card and George Gault proved to be mutually beneficial. The River Card seems to have stayed out of trouble and Gault's firm generated so much business off this deal that it had to issue the following statement on the River Card's website:

> We have reached our capacity for closing the contracts submitted, within the allocated time frame. However we will take care of those who have previously contacted us for closing or they have a pre-existing client/customer relationship with us.[17]

To his credit, the River Card knew that he was in over his head, and he also understood the importance of aligning himself with strategic partners who ingratiated themselves with his target market. George Gault not only understood the Texas Water Code, which would prove rather handy before all was said and done, but he also served as the city attorney for Mineral Wells. His connections and "wise and learned counsel" provided the credibility that the River Card would need to make this deal happen.

As for the lobbyists, the River Card put all of his eggs into the basket of Jay Propes from the Graydon Group, and for good reason. Make no mistake about this: Nothing happens in Austin without the leverage of a lobbyist and the Graydon Group came highly recommended. More importantly, Jay Propes had actually written Senate Bill 1326, which failed

---

17   Mike Patterson, "Approved Title Attorneys and Title Companies," *PK Land Partnership*, Patterson Equity Partners, n.d., accessed December 10, 2010. http://www.pklandpartnership.com/title.aspx.

to pass in 2007.[18] He rendered more or less the same service to the River Card for House Bill 3031.

During a presentation to the annual membership meeting of the Possum Kingdom Lake Association on June 23, 2007, Senator Estes' chief of staff, Lewis Simmons, "expressed the hope of Senator Estes that the relationship with the Graydon Group would continue into the future."[19] This statement warrants some explanation.

The Graydon Group entered the deal by serving as the lobbying firm for the Possum Kingdom Lake Preservation Association (PKLPA), a sister organization to the Possum Kingdom Lake Association (PKLA). Confusing, huh? It took me more than a while to sort this part out. Here's what you need to know about the PKLPA.

The Possum Kingdom Lake Preservation Association (PKLPA)

Fair warning: there is some rough water ahead. The Brazos River is one of the most meandering waterways in the United States, and if you look at a map, you will see that there are many places where it actually flows north. The same can be said for *The Tale of the River Card*.

If you are given to hard drink, this would be a good time to refill your glass. The next several pages will introduce a flood of characters and events. The primary intent is to paint a picture of the landscape that produced this deal. I would encourage you to simply take in the scenery and not worry just yet about what is around the next bend. When it comes time to focus in on the details, I will let you know.

As special interest groups go, the Possum Kingdom Lake Preservation Association is in a league of its own. The PKLPA's directors and members are not simply wealthy; they are superwealthy. We are talking about old oil

---

18   Phil Ford, "Substitute Revisions," e-mail message to Kenneth Anderson, Phil Wilson, March 26, 2007, accessed June 11, 2013.

19   "Annual Membership Meeting Summary," *Possum Kingdom Lake Association*, June 23, 2007, accessed December 12, 2010. http://www.pklakeassn.org/June%2023%20 Annual%20Meeting.htm.

money that is wrapped in a blanket of new natural gas money. And these folks don't simply wield political influence, they are kingmakers.

The modern-day Republican Party of Texas can trace a large portion of its roots to the Palo Pinto County area in general and specifically to one Chester Robert Upham Jr., who was known simply as Chet.

Chet Upham served as the state chairman of the Republican Party of Texas from 1979 to 1983; as a delegate to every Texas Republican convention from 1960 to 1994; as a delegate to the Republican National Convention in 1972, 1980, 1984, and 1992; and was a member of Governor Rick Perry's Business Council. He was also the founder of Upham Oil & Gas.

It is often said that before Chet Upham became involved, the Republican Party of Texas could fit into a phone booth. If you want to matriculate from state representative to state senator or from state senator to lieutenant governor, or from attorney general to governor, or from governor of Texas to the White House, then you will want the blessing and assistance of Chet Upham's political machine. The same is true if you simply want to save your job as the governor of Texas.

Chet's son Robert, formally Chester Robert Upham III, followed in his father's footsteps and now serves as the chief executive officer of Upham Oil & Gas. His chief financial officer, Mr. Paul McGettes, spends his spare time serving on the board of directors for First Financial Bank, alongside Representative Jim Keffer. During the battle over divestiture, Robert Upham also served as the chairman of the Possum Kingdom Lake Preservation Association (PKLPA).

And beyond all of that, Robert Upham also served as the chairman of the Brazos River Authority board of directors from 1987 to 1993. During his tenure, Possum Kingdom Lake effectively became a state-funded country club for the wealthy of Palo Pinto County. When the divestiture of the Brazos River Authority's property surrounding Possum Kingdom Lake became an Upham family project, it became a priority for Governor Perry and his lieutenants.

On the same evening that Lewis Simmons informed the PKLA that Senator Estes wanted the Graydon Group to remain on the payroll, Mr. Joe Shannon also addressed the group as the director of communications for the PKLPA. His comments were intended to help the weekenders understand that if they wanted the help of the Republican hierarchy, then they would need to learn how to play some political poker.

The meeting minutes of the PKLA recorded the following:

> Finally, Mr. Joe Shannon spoke to the Association as Director of Communications for the PK [Lake] Preservation Association. Shannon served three terms in the Texas House of Representatives and immediately after his final session as a Representative, served as Administrative Assistant to the Speaker of the House. Shannon spoke of the importance of supporting our elected officials in "even-numbered years and not just in odd-numbered years." He noted that it was very important for our members to support both financially and with campaign efforts those legislators who seek reelection and who have been helpful to the Association's efforts in Austin. Shannon emphasized the importance of continuing our efforts over the next 14–18 months before the next session. He stated that efforts to obtain favorable legislation must be continuous and that our Association must not lessen its efforts toward divestiture because we are between sessions of the Legislature. He stated his opinion that the Legislature is a very powerful force and that the BRA has most likely realized that fact.

Few people can speak to the *powerful force* that is the Texas legislature better than Joe Shannon. After his service as a state representative from 1964 to 1971, he ran for the state senate and lost. Fortunately for his career, he was offered and accepted a position as an administrative assistant to the Texas Speaker of the House. Unfortunately for his career, that gentleman's name was Gus Mutscher Jr., who is widely considered to be one of the most corrupt House Speakers in the history of Texas. And that is saying something.

In the fall of 1971, Speaker Mutscher, Speaker pro tem Tommy Shannon (no relation to Joe Shannon), and an aide to Mutscher by the name of Rush McGinty were indicted on a felony charge that alleged that the three men had conspired to accept a bribe from a Houston banker by the name of Frank W. Sharp. The indictment arose from a lawsuit filed by the SEC in a federal court in Dallas related to what is now known as the Sharpstown stock-fraud scandal that hit Austin like an earthquake.

The crux of the matter alleged that Mutscher and the others were loaned $600,000 by Frank Sharp's bank so that they could buy stock in his insurance company in exchange for favorable legislation that would benefit Sharp's business interests. After the stock was purchased, the SEC alleged that Sharp artificially inflated the value of the stock and that everyone involved made out like bandits.

To put the Sharpstown stock-fraud scandal into perspective, $600,000 in 1972 would equate to roughly $3 million in 2009. Although the parallels between *The Tale of the River Card* and the Sharpstown stock-fraud scandal are alarmingly numerous, the former dwarfs the latter in both the dollar terms and the elected officials involved. The scam related to *The Tale of the River Card* was one hundred times that of the Sharpstown stock-fraud scandal. Consider that one reason to keep on reading.

It took an Abilene jury only 140 minutes to find Mutscher and his codefendants guilty of the charge after considering "hundreds of pounds and hours of evidence."[20] At the defendants' request, punishment was imposed by the judge rather than the jury. On March 16, 1972, Judge J. Neil Daniel slapped House Speaker Mutscher, Speaker pro tem Shannon, and the Speaker's aide McGinty with five years of hard probation.[21] Nonetheless, the landscape of politics in Texas was forever changed as the boat wake from the scandal swept all the way to the governor's mansion. Afterwards, the politicians in Texas were forced to get craftier in their craft.

During the trial, Joe Shannon served as the defense counsel for Tommy Shannon and cited the case, on his official website, as one of the most notable of his career. This same website also states that he served as the administrative assistant to the Speaker of the House of Texas from 1971 to 1972.[22] It would seem that while Joe Shannon was defending one of Speaker Mutscher's codefendants, he was also on Speaker Mutscher's state payroll. By the way, that official website is for the district attorney of Tarrant County, the Honorable Joe Shannon. And please make a note that Tarrant County is where the River Card was born and raised.

---

20   Sam Kinch Jr., "Sharpstown Stock-Fraud Scandal," *Handbook of Texas Online*, Texas State Historical Association, n.d., accessed February 1, 2011. http://www.tshaonline. org/handbook/online/articles/mqs01.

21   We elect our judges in Texas.

22   "About Joe Shannon," *Office of the Tarrant County DA*, n.p., n.d., accessed November 25, 2011. http://www.joeshannonda.com/resume.asp.

After Mutscher resigned in 1972, Joe Shannon returned to Fort Worth and took a chief's position in the Tarrant County district attorney's office, working for a gentleman that he had grown up with. That fellow's name was Tim Curry.

Joe Shannon and Tim Curry worked together until 1978, and their experience together was highlighted by their case against Richard "Racehorse" Haynes in one of the most expensive and highly publicized murder trials in the history of Texas. That trial accused oilman Cullen Davis of murdering his estranged wife and a few others. After fourteen months of testimony, Cullen Davis was acquitted of all charges and set free. Joe Shannon went into private practice the next year.

Joe Shannon returned to the Tarrant County district attorney's office in 1999, again working for Tim Curry. During this second tour of duty, his career took another fortuitous turn just a few days before Governor Perry signed HB 3031 into law. Following Mr. Curry's death in April 2009, Joe Shannon received a promotion. As reported by Eric Griffey of the *Fort Worth Weekly*, here is how it happened:

> So when Curry passed away in April, after a long battle with lung cancer, it wasn't a big surprise when Shannon was named to succeed him—except to Shannon himself, at least the way he tells it.
>
> He wasn't planning on putting his name in the hat, Shannon told a group of journalists recently, until aides to Gov. Rick Perry encouraged him to do so. Even then, he didn't think his application would be taken seriously, he said, because he waited until the last possible minute to apply.
>
> He was at a conference in New Orleans not long after that, when one of Perry's people called. The governor needed to meet with him the next day. On no sleep, he flew to Austin, arrived early, and sat in the waiting area of the governor's office. But instead of meeting with Perry, Shannon got the news from a staffer: He had the job, without ever having been interviewed or spoken a word with Perry about it.[23]

---

23   Eric Griffey, "Cut From the Same Cloth," *Fort Worth Weekly*, July 15, 2009, accessed February 1, 2014. http://www.fwweekly.com/2009/07/15/cut-from-the-same-cloth.

In the spring of 2009, unemployment in the United States was approaching 10 percent, yet Joe Shannon landed a premium job that he wasn't even looking for. As you will see, good things tend to happen to people who spend their weekends at Possum Kingdom Lake and do business with the Graydon Group.

Of course, doing business with the Graydon Group does not make you immune to civil litigation. In March 2012, one of Joe Shannon's assistant district attorneys, Sabrina Sabin, filed a sexual harassment complaint against him, alleging "conduct that went on from 2008 until January 2012 and made her life 'unbearable.'"[24] This would mean that the conduct in question began before Governor Perry appointed Joe Shannon to replace Tim Curry in 2009.

While the allegations against Joe Shannon are unfit for print here, fairness requires that it be noted that he denied the allegations. Nonetheless, Tarrant County settled the matter for $375,000 in September 2013. Shortly thereafter, Shannon informed his staff by e-mail that he would not seek reelection and that he would retire at the beginning of 2015.[25]

The Possum Kingdom Lake Association (PKLA)

Without the Possum Kingdom Lake Association, there would be no River Card. As every cardsharp knows, you can't cheat an honest man. That is not to say that the PKLA is a dishonest bunch of folks, only that they live by a different set of rules than the rest of us. While the majority of us complain that politicians pander to special-interest groups, they complain that the hired help doesn't pander fast enough. And by "hired help" I do mean politicians.

The River Card characterized the PKLA as "cautious, careful, and always having the best of intentions." To say the least, this assessment is questionable. The River Card closed his tribute to the unsung heroes by thanking the president of the PKLA and his wife "for all you both continue to do for us all!" He was referring to Monte and Carolyn Land, and these

---

24 Tim Madigan, "I Was Sexually Harassed by Joe Shannon, District Attorney," *Fort Worth Star-Telegram*, January 26, 2013, accessed February 1, 2014. http://www.star-telegram.com/2013/01/25/4576466/allegations-detailed-i-was-sexually.html.

25 Max B. Baker, "Tarrant County DA Says He Would Have Won Re-election, But Chose to Retire Instead," *Fort Worth Star-Telegram*, October 1, 2013, accessed February 1, 2014. http://www.star-telegram.com/2013/10/01/5211180/tarrant-county-district-attorney.html.

were rather kind words, considering that the River Card and the PKLA were not exactly on speaking terms.

To circumvent the Texas Constitution and several statutory laws, the PKLA and the PKLPA had to have a straw man in order to purchase the land under their homes at a deep discount. The River Card had positioned himself as their only option, and he reminded Monte Land of this fact in an e-mail dated August 31, 2009:

> Dear Monte [...]
>
> I understand why you filed the lawsuit before HB 3031 became law, but question why you and the PKLA now are still pursuing this appeal since HB 3031 has become law.
>
> If successful I have to assume, unless you tell me otherwise, that you would also ask for all subsequent tax years, including 2008, to be reappraised. [...]
>
> Please remember that if I am not successful in my effort to purchase the leaseholds from the BRA because of this lawsuit, the PK BRA leaseholders will not be buying from me at a % of their 2008 land assessed tax values, but rather per HB 3031 purchasing directly from the BRA at whatever the then current tax assessed land value is (2010 value?). [...]
>
> Monte, I know you have good and honorable intentions, so please carefully consider the possible ramifications of your lawsuit. I believed you when you announced at the last PKLA annual meeting that you support my purchase effort. If not stopped, this kind of legal action could spook my investors and lenders. You can be very helpful to me now by not chasing this rabbit down this rabbit trail.
>
> Even if you were successful in your lawsuit, and some judge and/ or jury were to say "The PK leaseholders should get their lots for $800 a piece", and that ruling caused me not to be able to close by my deadline of December 31, 2010, I very much doubt that the PK BRA lessees would be able to purchase from the BRA their lots at the values you suggest. Remember the next legislative session starts the very next month in January of 2011. I doubt that the BRA and the Texas Legislature would ever let us buy our lots any cheaper than the opportunity we have right now.

Mike[26]

We will be examining the lawsuit to which the River Card referred in due course. We will also take a hard look at those 2008 tax values. But for the time being, let's focus on this e-mail exchange. The next day, the River Card complained to the Mineral Wells Index that he did not understand the motives of the PKLA and would gladly pay $100,000 to make them go away.[27] One week later, Monte Land put the River Card on notice that he would determine the future course of events.

> Mike,
>
> I have passed on this letter of request regarding our lawsuit with the appraisal district to our lawyers and they indicated to me they will respond if they feel it necessary. They both asked that if you had any questions or need any further explanation regarding this matter to contact either of them. They would be Robert Aldrich and Greg Fitzgerald.
>
> Monte[28]

The bad blood that developed between the River Card and the leadership of the PKLA would eventually melt away when everyone had what they wanted. However, neither the PKLA nor the River Card seemed to understand that their less than private feud was leaving a blood trail in the water. That blood trail was now attracting sharks. The types of people who had exposed the Texas rent-to-own scandal were now taking notes.

---

26 Mike Patterson, "09/10/2009 Email RE: Monte J. Land et al v. Palo Pinto Appraisal District-lawsuit challenging PK BRA leasehold valuation methodology," *Patterson PK Land Partnership Ltd.* n.d., accessed April 1, 2010. http://www.pklandpartnership.com/09_10_09.aspx.

27 Libby Cluett, "Lawsuit Go Buy-Bye?" *Mineral Wells Index*, September 21, 2009, accessed February 1, 2012. http://mineralwellsindex.com/local/x20311479/-font-color-blue-Brazos-River-Authority-DIVESTITURE-font-Lawsuit-go-buy-bye/print.

28 Monte Land "09/10/2009 Email RE: Monte J. Land et al v. Palo Pinto Appraisal District-lawsuit challenging PK BRA leasehold valuation methodology" *Patterson PK Land Partnership Ltd.* n.d., accessed April 1, 2010. http://www.pklandpartnership.com/09_10_09.aspx.

Monte and Carolyn Land also provided an invaluable public service. Like the River Card, they were kind enough to tell this story in their own words by publishing their meeting minutes to the Internet without so much as the restriction of a copyright. As a result, they have no reasonable expectation of privacy and the rest of us are entitled to their enlightenments.[29]

The Other People

To say the least, the River Card's collection of unsung heroes is an interesting group of folks. It is hard not to notice, however, that the River Card had just bid $50 million to buy a portfolio of lakefront property, yet he needed funding for the first $2.5 million in earnest money. The obvious conclusion is that he bought almost $1 billion worth of property using $50 million worth of other people's money.

Speaking of other people, there are a few names on our list of unsung heroes that have not yet been categorized, as their relationship to the River Card is less than obvious. Take for example Ms. Rebecca Lucas, whom the River Card described as providing "always unwavering support."

Ms. Lucas is an attorney in Fort Worth who served on the Fort Worth Ethics Commission during the Possum Kingdom land grab. On December 16, 2005, Ms. Lucas submitted the following question to the Brazos River Authority:

> I have read the Shoreline Management Manual. I think the requirement of matching names on boat and leases to avoid a user fee deserves another look. I have been with my companion, Joe Shannon for almost 10 years. He paid for 1/2 of the dock. We are not married however, and because I own the leasehold on the property, he bought the boat. You could very easily write a 'partnership' exception into the rule whereby we could file an affidavit with the BRA that his use of the lease matches mine, or that we are partners in the boat—we should not have to change

---

29　My lawyers insist that I point this out at every opportunity. The Possum Kingdom Lake Association's Meeting Minutes are presented in PlayingPossum.org.

the title on the boat or transfer it to me—your language simply is too broad, but the cure should be easy.[30]

It would seem that "unwavering support" and marital commitment are less than synonymous. This is understandable, however, in the case of Tarrant County district attorney, Joe Shannon. If you have ever seen the movie *Charlie Wilson's War*, you might remember a scene where a woman named Carol Shannon performed a belly dance for the defense minister of Egypt. The objective of the performance was to persuade the minister to provide arms to Afghanistan in that country's war against the Soviet Union. Carol Shannon was the former Mrs. Joe Shannon, and she met Charlie Wilson while she and Joe were still married. The rest of the story, as they say, is an odd piece of Texas history.

In December 2007, Ms. Lucas was also one of three leaseholders who petitioned Attorney General Greg Abbott to find in favor of the concerned lessees of Possum Kingdom Lake. This letter was crafted by Attorney James D. Shields and asserted that the lessees had invested in their leaseholds based on an expectation that the lease rates would remain negligible. As it turned out, they had bet wrong.

Another amusing entry in the category of "other people" is Mark Engebretson with the *Lake Country Sun*. "Mark has been tireless and has kept up the necessary coverage to keep all of us adequately informed."[31] Considering that the River Card's lobbyist, Jay Propes, was intimately involved in the drafting and crafting of HB 3031, it is difficult to believe that his primary source of information was coming from a rural newspaper.[32]

While it would be easier to believe that Mark Engebretson served as the River Card's spin machine at the lake, questioning the integrity of a mainstream journalist could invite adverse repercussions. Consequently, this might be the last that you hear of the *Lake Country Sun*. To avoid

---

30   Rebecca C. Lucas, "PK Shoreline Management Comments," *Brazos River Authority*, December 16, 2005, accessed February 1, 2014. http://www.brazos.org/generalPdf/PKShorelineManagementPublicComments.pdf.

31   Mike Patterson, "Unsung Heroes," *PK Land Partnership*, Patterson Equity Partners, n.d., accessed February 1, 2010.

32   Get used to the term "intimately involved in the drafting and crafting of HB 3031." For legal reasons, it would be premature to state who actually wrote House Bill 3031.

the appearance of total cowardice in the face of the power of the media, exhaustive research has revealed that Mark Engebretson is Facebook friends with Marsha Bettis. Ms. Bettis is a real estate agent at Possum Kingdom Lake and was also credited as an "unsung hero" who provided "always unwavering support." She is also not hard to look at.

Seriously speaking, one of the greatest lessons of *The Tale of the River Card* surrounds the progressive demise of the investigative journalist. When traditional printed newspapers began to lose ad revenue to online competitors, they were no longer able to employ the likes of Woodward and Bernstein with open-ended budgets. As a result, politicians nationwide can engage in deals of this nature with relative impunity. There are simply very few watchdogs left watching.

Lance Byrd

While most of our unsung heroes played a supporting role, Lance Byrd stands alone as the catalyst for the River Card's entry into the game. As a reminder, the River Card put it this way in the opening of his thank-you note:

> Lance Byrd—He was my inspiration to get involved. I watched from the sidelines in 2007 as he, with the help of a few, almost pushed divestiture to the goal line in the 80th legislative session. His leadership and determination inspired me to get involved.

Mr. Lance R. Byrd is the president and CEO of Sendero Energy. He is also on the board of directors of the AT&T Cotton Bowl, which tells you that he has some serious stroke in North Texas.[33] He was also on Governor Rick Perry's financial leadership team when Kay Bailey Hutchison was mounting her challenge and the River Card was making his play.[34]

Evidently, Lance is also a dude who likes to party. Mr. Byrd and his wife acquired their property at Possum Kingdom Lake on April 29, 2002, and received the following letter a few years later.

---

33 AT&T Cotton Bowl Board of Directors, *AT&T Cotton Bowl*, n.p., n.d., accessed February 1, 2014. http://www.attcottonbowl.com/contact-us/att-cotton-bowl-board/.

34 "Perry Announces Finance Leadership for 2010 Gubernatorial Campaign," *Texans for Rick Perry,* June 29, 2009, accessed February 1, 2014. http://www.rickperry.org/release/perry-announces-finance-leadership-2010-gubernatorial-campaign.

October 7, 2004

Mr. and Mrs. Lance R. Byrd
2626 Cole Avenue, Suite 500
Dallas, Texas 75204

Re: Violation of Lease

Dear Mr. and Mrs. Byrd:

I have been advised of recent police reports requiring Brazos River Authority officers to respond to disturbances connected to your property. This activity is a violation of Paragraph 9 (lessee shall not conduct any activity which in the opinion of Authority is improper, immoral, noxious, annoying, creates a nuisance) of your lease agreement, Section 16 of the Rules for Governance of Brazos River Authority (No disorderly, noxious, disruptive or offensive activity shall be conducted on the Lakes or on Authority lands.), and Texas Penal Code, Section 42.01, Disorderly Conduct, paragraph (a), (5) makes unreasonable noise in a public place other that a sport shooting range (copies enclosed for your review). [*sic*]

I take this type of inappropriate activity very seriously. Continued activity of this nature could be justifiable cause for cancellation of your lease agreement. I look forward to your cooperation helping me ensure this lake remains a retreat for all to enjoy.

I sincerely hope that this situation does not reoccur.

Very truly yours,

MICHAEL J. ILTIS

Area Project Manager

MJI/gmc

    Cc: Mike Cox, Area Chief Lake Ranger

        Kent Rindy, Upper Basin Region Manager

        Lauralee Vallon, Executive Counsel[35]

Now, understand that if the BRA cancels your lease for cause, your party is over. More importantly, anything that you have built on the land becomes the property of the BRA. Since Lance Byrd had just built

---

35   Michael J. Iltis, "Re: Violation of Lease," letter to Mr. and Mrs. Lance R. Byrd, October 7, 2004, accessed March 4, 2010. http://www.pklandpartnership.com/brafiles/1-23_5-2-31_U/Correspondence/1_23_5_2_31_U_Correspondence.pdf.

a three-story lakefront home at 2963 Colonel's Row, valued by the Palo Pinto Appraisal District at roughly $800,000, he might have considered the loss of a $1 million estate a rather harsh penalty for a few minor party fouls. It is not hard to understand why he became the driving force behind divestiture.

Having learned his lesson about throwing wild parties, Byrd sent a letter to the Brazos River Authority on May 19, 2006, and copied the local chief of police, Mike Cox. Byrd's letter requested permission to throw a party on Sunday, July 17, featuring Cross Canadian Ragweed, a country/rock band. His anticipated guest list was approximately 175 people. He assured the Brazos River Authority that no alcohol would be sold, that no underage individuals would be served, and that all of the youngsters would be accompanied by their parents. On June 16, 2008, Byrd sent a similar letter requesting to throw yet another party on July 12 with the same format, featuring Reckless Kelly. On both occasions, he received a groveling approval from the BRA. I suppose that the Texas legislature is indeed a force that is powerful enough to change attitudes.

To say the least, the River Card's collection of unsung heroes was a colorful lot. This brings us to the next most obvious question:

Who the hell is the River Card?

Chapter 3

THE RIVER CARD

Michael Patterson, a.k.a. the River Card, was born and raised in Arlington, Texas. For those of you who are not familiar with this area, Arlington is now the home of both the Dallas Cowboys and the Texas Rangers.

The Arlington distinction is an important one. *The Tale of the River Card* is not simply another yarn about tycoons from Dallas and Fort Worth exploiting the system. Make no mistake about it: there are plenty of folks from those locales involved in this tale, but this is a story about a good old boy from Arlington, making his play and making it big.

Arlington, Texas, enjoys its own economic and social universe. The Arlington Chamber of Commerce is a major force in the area and so too is an organization known as the Margarita Society. You can rest assured that the people in Arlington know how to craft a deal, as evidenced by the fact that both the Texas Rangers and the Dallas Cowboys used to belong to someone else.

The River Card is a hard guy to figure out. He is a lawyer so proficient in his craft that he was able to beat the state of Texas out of roughly $40 million almost overnight. Simultaneously, he is an attorney who is so careless that he published a stockpile of his working papers, e-mails, and audio recordings on the Internet without so much as the protection of a copyright.[36]

For example, the letter from the Brazos River Authority to Mr. and Mrs. Lance Byrd threatening to terminate their lease would ordinarily be considered a private matter. But, because the letter was written on the BRA's stationery and published to the Internet by the River Card for anyone to access; the letter is now part of the public domain. If Mr. Byrd has a problem with that, he will need to take it up with his friend Michael Patterson—a.k.a. the River Card.[37]

The River Card's father was Harold E. Patterson who was born at the beginning of the Great Depression and was the youngest of fourteen children. Harold was widely held as a man of sound integrity, who rose from the ranks of a bank teller to eventually own four banks, with mixed results. He was also the former mayor of Arlington, and he was often referred to as "Mr. Arlington."

In fact, two days before the River Card submitted his winning bid to purchase the property surrounding Possum Kingdom Lake, the Texas Senate memorialized Mr. Arlington in a resolution that was crafted by Senators Wendy Davis and Chris Harris.[38] To make a long story short, the River Card grew up around politicians and bankers, and his gift for navigating the political and financial waters was well incubated.

In contrast, most of the River Card's career was unremarkable. He had never completed a major real estate transaction in his life, and he had never led a private equity investment. To his credit, he informed his potential investors of this fact in the "private placement memorandum" that was used to finance the equity portion of his deal.

Lack of experience operating a business similar to that of the Partnership. Although certain affiliates of the General Partner have considerable experience in the commercial real estate industry

---

36   My lawyers are going to make a fortune defending me in court some day. Of course, if someone is bold enough to file a punitive lawsuit, that will open up the discovery process and the real fun will begin.

37   You can rest assured that certain journalists and investigative reporters have already downloaded this Internet file and all of the others to their laptops.

38   "Senate Journal," *Eighty-First Legislature–Regular Session*, Texas Senate, April 6, 2009, p. 898.

in general, the General Partner and its affiliates have no significant experience in real estate acquisition, sale, leasing and management of the kind contemplated by the Partnership. Therefore, the General Partner and its affiliates have no prior performance or track record of returns resulting from the formation of an entity to acquire residential and commercial real estate and the operation, management, lease, and sale of such properties upon which to judge whether the Partnership's business strategy will be successful or that the General Partner and its affiliates will be effective in carrying out such business strategy.[39]

So at least the River Card told the truth about his talents and his background. Let me do the same about the rest of it.

Michael Patterson is and was the principal of Peirson Patterson, LLP. The stock and trade of this firm is creating loan documents. Assume that you are a small community bank in Texas, and assume further that you do not possess the technological sophistication required to convert your own customers' data into loan documents. Your solution is to send your customers' data to Peirson Patterson, LLP, and they will do it for you.

Since this is *The Tale of the River Card*, it seems fair to allow him to characterize his pedigree in his own words. The following is his profile from the Patterson Equity Partners website that was launched right after he won the bid to purchase the property.

> Michael H. Patterson serves as the sole manager of the General Partner. Mr. Patterson also maintains a commercial real estate law practice in Arlington, Texas (Peirson Patterson, LLP). Within such practice, Mr. Patterson has over 10 years of experience representing various real estate developers, contractors and title companies in the Dallas-Fort Worth Metroplex and has over 25 years of experience in preparing and negotiating national residential real estate loan documents and addressing related compliance matters. Mr. Patterson has served as a director of Southwest Securities, FSB for over 10 years and has nearly 20 years of experience with various civic organizations in Arlington, Texas, including the Arlington

---

39   Mike Patterson, "Private Placement Memorandum, Risk Factors," *PK Land Partnership*, Patterson Equity Partners, September 30, 2009, accessed February 1, 2010. http://www. pklandpartnership.com/downloads/1%20of%203%20-%20Final%20as%20of%20 9-30-09.pdf.

Independent School District and the Arlington Planning and Zoning Commission. Mr. Patterson holds a Bachelor of Business Administration degree from Southern Methodist University and a law degree from the University of Texas at Austin.[40]

This is the guy who beat Governor Rick Perry and the state of Texas out of a small fortune?

While it is true that the River Card had served on the board of Southwest Securities, FSB, for over ten years, his days in that capacity were numbered. A few years earlier, the bank's holding company had hired a new president, John Holt, to overhaul the bank and its dysfunctional board. Not long after the River Card won the bid to purchase the lakefront property, he was removed from the board of Southwest Securities, FSB. Nonetheless, the River Card left this credential on his investment website for a substantial period of time after his departure.

It has been said that behind every good man there is a good woman, but the original Mrs. Patterson had absolutely nothing to do with this deal. In fact, shortly after the River Card made his first, last, and only multimillion-dollar score, he walked out on his wife of nearly thirty years. The divorce was final on February 17, 2011, and the River Card married an attorney who had been working for his law firm on May 15, 2011. If you care about this sort of thing, the River Card got ten years younger at that position. He deeded his home at 2929 Colonel's Row on Possum Kingdom Lake to the former Mrs. Patterson on September 1, 2011.

Rather than relying on the support of a good woman, the River Card enjoyed the services of a young lad by the name of Jarod Cox. Again, we can refer to the River Card's website for an explanation of who Jarod Cox is.

> Jarod Cox serves as Director for the partnership. Mr. Cox recently served as a Special Assistant to a Texas State Senator from December 2006 through January 2009. Prior to such service, Mr. Cox worked as a Senior Associate for Encore Acquisition Company in Fort Worth, Texas from June 2006 to December

---

40   Michael Patterson, "Our Team," *PK Land Partnership*, Patterson Equity Partners, n.d., accessed March 5, 2010. http://www.pattersonequitypartners.com/about-patterson-equity/patterson-equity-team/.

2006 and as a Senior Associate for KPMG LLP in Fort Worth,
Texas from September 2004 to June 2006. Mr. Cox holds a Master
of Accountancy degree and a Bachelors of Business Administration
in Accounting degree from Abilene Christian University.[41]

Whoa up. Name-dropping is an art form in Texas politics, and
when a young gun tells you that he used to work for a nameless state
senator, something is wrong. As it turns out, Mr. Cox's former employer
is a gentleman by the name of Kim Brimer, who was previously the state
senator from District 10, which included Arlington, Texas.[42]

Were it not for former state senator Kim Brimer and his real estate
scandal, it is highly unlikely that anyone would have ever heard of an
obscure councilwoman from Fort Worth by the name of Wendy Russell
Davis.

In 2008, a female Democrat, whose middle name is Russell, challenged
a male Republican, who went by the name of Kim, for the senate seat in
District 10. The Republican was the incumbent, and he had won his
previous two elections in 2002 and 2004 by a tally of 60 percent to 40
percent, respectively, against his Democratic challengers.

Senate District 10 was a Republican stronghold, yet Kim Brimer lost
to a woman who had never served a single day in the Texas legislature. In
fact, he was the only Republican in the thirty-one–member chamber of
the Senate to lose his seat to a Democrat in the general election that year.
Sometimes winning an election is not actually about winning. Instead, it
is about having enough prescience to be on the ballot when the incumbent
loses.

Not to take anything away from Ms. Davis, but Senator Kim
Brimer did indeed lose his Senate seat in 2008. While he pulled 47.52
percent of the vote, Wendy Davis pulled 49.94 percent, producing a
2.5 percent margin of victory. Yes, she was articulate, and yes, she was
an intriguing, attractive, and compelling candidate. But there is no

---

41   Michael Patterson, "Our Team," *PK Land Partnership*, Patterson Equity Partners,
     n.d., accessed March 5, 2010. http://www.pattersonequitypartners.com/
     about-patterson-equity/patterson-equity-team/.

42   That is not a misprint. The man's name is Kim, and his hairdo makes former Dallas
     Cowboys coach Jimmy Johnson look like he is sporting a crew cut. His formal name is
     Kenneth Kimberlin Brimer Jr.

way on God's green earth that Wendy Davis should have ever won that election.

Nonetheless, she did win, and a new chapter in Texas history was set in motion. Here is how that happened.

Senator Kim Brimer purchased a residence outside of Austin and put the property in his wife's name. He then used money from his campaign coffers to pay his wife rent on the place so that he could stay there while he was in Austin, conducting business for the state of Texas. The rent payments were enough to cover the mortgage payments and then some. When all was said and done, Senator Brimer and his wife would own the property outright.

Unfortunately for Senator Brimer, his real estate deal became known as the "rent-to-own scandal," and even the most hard-core Republicans in District 10 were taken aback by his brazen abuse of the system. Enter Wendy Russell Davis, who seems to be a delightful young lady that I hope to have the opportunity to meet some day.

If we reflect back on the River Card's thank-you note, we are reminded that he characterized himself as a "little duck that seems to glide effortlessly across the pond." While it would be rude to counter this portrayal by referring to the River Card as a shark that was preying on the greed of others, it is fair to say that he served as an excellent financial benchmark for the true value of the land that was sold.

On November 5, 2008, Richard Ellis, an appraiser from Mineral Wells, provided an appraisal of the River Card's lakefront property to Affiliated Bank in Arlington. This appraisal valued the four-tenths of an acre of dirt beneath the River Card's home at $350,000. By contrast, the Palo Pinto Appraisal District *assessed* the value of this same dirt in 2008 at $65,560. If we take these numbers as gospel, then the River Card's property was actually worth five times more than the assessed value. If we use these numbers as a benchmark, then the entire twelve hundred acres of shoreline that was sold was actually worth roughly $977 million.

Let's make the math easy and round that number up to $1 billion.

We should probably perform a sanity check on these numbers. The River Card paid $50 million for the entire inhabited shoreline of one of the most pristine lakes in the state of Texas. That comes out to roughly $42,000 per acre for the lakefront property. That seems a bit cheap to me.

On the other hand, the River Card's appraiser put the value of an acre of lakefront property at over $800,000. That seems about right to me, so I am going to stick with this math until someone can convince me otherwise. All that is required to prove me wrong is to aggregate all of the appraisals that were performed when the leaseholders financed their lots through the River Card's preferred lenders.

It would seem that the Palo Pinto Appraisal District agreed with the River Card's appraiser. On May 3, 2008, the River Card and his former wife were notified by the PPAD that the assessed value of their property had increased from $65,560 to $318,430.[43] For years, the property taxes on the lakefront property had been ridiculously low, and the chief appraiser in Palo Pinto County was trying to get the pot right. Her name was Donna Rhoades. The River Card's 2008 assessed value put the price of an acre of lakefront property right at $750,000.

Unfortunately, Ms. Rhoades's efforts to bring the property taxes on the lakefront property up to par were in vain. The Palo Pinto Appraisal District only had $30,000 budgeted for legal fees in 2008, and they received an avalanche of protests and petitions.[44] As a result, Chief Appraiser Rhoades had no choice but to roll the increases back to the 2007 values. Keep this fact in mind.

If you remember that little e-mail ass-tangle between the River Card and the president of the PKLA, the topic of discussion was an outstanding lawsuit against Donna Rhoades concerning the methodology that was used to determine the assessed values. The River Card was trying desperately to convince Monte Land that it was time to declare victory and move on. He also tried to explain that the 2008 values were actually the same as the 2007 values and that the price was only going to go up—and go up dramatically. Here is how the River Card put it:

> As a lessee I am very happy with my opportunity to buy my land
> at the present 2008 land tax assessed value. The final PK BRA

43   Mike Patterson, "Notice of Appraised Value," *PK Land Partnership*, Patterson Equity Partners, May 3, 2008, accessed February 1, 2010. http://www.pklandpartnership.com/downloads/PK%20BRA%205.pdf.

44   Libby Cluett, "Appraisal District's Legal Fees Rise with PK Lawsuits," *Mineral Wells Index*, September 17, 2008, accessed February 1, 2012. http://mineralwellsindex.com/local/x154988179/Appraisal-district-s-legal-fees-rise-with-PK-lawsuits/print.

2008 land values were very close to the 2007 land values. Mine was the exact same, $65,000.00. Do we really want to invite all the leaseholds to be reappraised?

A lot of good people (including yourself) have worked very hard so we can all have a chance to buy our lots at a very reasonable price.

Palo Pinto Chief Appraiser, Donna Rhoades came very close to substantially raising our 2008 tax values, but decided otherwise due to the uncertainty of leasehold renewals at the time:

http://www.pklandpartnership.com/downloads/PK%20 BRA%206.pdf

That uncertainty is now gone. We now have multiple and very clear lease and purchase options based upon 2008 tax assessed land values. I am guessing that is why a lot of our 2009 taxed assessed land values have jumped up so high. My 2009 land tax value is more than twice my 2008 land tax value.[45]

To be precise, the River Card's final 2009 tax assessment on the property at 2929 Colonel's Row was $149,850. I use the term "final" because the original tax assessment that was sent out on April 29, 2009, had once again attempted to set the assessment at $318,430.[46] Coincidentally, the original 2009 assessment was sent out the day after the BRA voted to accept the River Card's bid. If you have never bothered to challenge your property taxes because you don't think it would be worth the trouble, then you might want to revisit that topic.

As I understand things so far, the River Card paid five cents on the dollar for the entire inhabited shoreline of a lake with the obligation to resell the property for nine cents on the dollar.

How could this possibly have been legal?

---

45 Mike Patterson, "09/10/2009 E-mail RE: Monte J. Land et al. v. Palo Pinto Appraisal District-lawsuit challenging PK BRA leasehold valuation methodology" *Patterson PK Land Partnership, LTD.* n.d., accessed April 1, 2010. http://www.pklandpartnership. com/09_10_09.aspx.

46 Mike Patterson, "Notice of Appraised Value," *PK Land Partnership*, Patterson Equity Partners, May 7, 2009, accessed February 1, 2010. http://www.pklandpartnership.com/ downloads/PK%20BRA%2012.pdf.

Chapter 4

THE LAW OF THE LAND

For the sake of full disclosure, I have to confess that I am among those who do not care about the sale of surplus real estate in Palo Pinto County. Fifty-million-dollar real estate deals are a dime a dozen in the state of Texas and so too are the people who put them together. And as a devoted poker player, my only response to someone staking $50 million and winning a $1 billion pot is this: "That's a hand well played, sir."

On the other hand, there is a suggestion on the table that someone may have gotten somewhat raped along the way. Even I would have to admit that such an act would be somewhat scandalous, so you can color me somewhat interested. I also have to acknowledge that betting $50 million that you *don't* have, in a game that is run by politicians, is a ballsy move. So you can color me even more interested. But if you really want me to give a possum's ass about your deal, you are going to have to convince me that you broke a few laws and maybe a few marriage vows along the way. Having limited experience with infidelity, up to and including the mistreatment of goats, my opening interest concerns the law.

Constitutionality

Article III, Section 52, of the Texas Constitution prevents the Texas legislature from granting a gratuitous gift to any individual or group of individuals. Specifically, the text states:

> The Legislature shall have no power to authorize any county, city, town or other political corporation or subdivision of the State to lend its credit or to grant public money or thing of value in aid of, or to any individual, association or corporation whatsoever.

The state of Texas frowns upon people who practice law without a license, so I am going to resist the temptation to advise you that selling $1 billion worth of prime Texas real estate well below fair market value constitutes "granting a thing of value." I will tell you, however, that in September 1998, Democratic attorney general Dan Morales declared exactly that in Opinion 98-082. I can also tell you that in June 2008, Republican Attorney General Greg Abbott declared exactly the opposite in Opinion AG-0634. In the years since those opinions were rendered, Attorney General Morales has spent time in a federal penitentiary for conspiracy, while Attorney General Greg Abbott, who is now running for governor of the state of Texas, has not. So who are we to believe here?

Question 1 on the table is whether or not the real estate in question was sold for something significantly less than fair market value. Question 2 on the table is whether or not violating the Texas Constitution is actually a crime. While a person of average intelligence can determine the answer to question 1, only a legal scholar can definitively answer question 2.

Bribery

You may or may not be surprised to learn that the Texas Penal Code prohibits bribing a public official. Title 8 of the Texas Penal Code is entitled "Offenses against Public Administration."

Chapter 36 under Title 8 addresses "Bribery and Corrupt Influence." Specifically, this text states:

> Sec. 36.02. BRIBERY. (a) A person commits an offense if he intentionally or knowingly offers, confers, or agrees to confer on another, or solicits, accepts, or agrees to accept from another:

(1) any benefit as consideration for the recipient's decision, opinion, recommendation, vote, or other exercise of discretion as a public servant, party official, or voter;

(2) any benefit as consideration for the recipient's decision, vote, recommendation, or other exercise of official discretion in a judicial or administrative proceeding;

In Texas, you could say that bribery is in the eye of the beholder. If no money changes hands, then maybe all that you have is some good old-fashioned horse trading, which is considered a noble art form in these parts. Or maybe it isn't.

To prove a charge of bribery in Texas, you typically need a paper trail that involves something other than campaign contributions. Generally speaking, there are no limits on how much an individual can contribute to a candidate's campaign in Texas. Consequently, there was nothing to prevent the River Card from throwing money around like Bo Pilgrim, which he did.[47]

On the other hand, public servants who are appointed by the governor have no campaign coffers to stuff money into. As a result, these individuals require much more creative forms of motivation. This is where *quid pro quo* comes into play. Assume, for example, that an individual might have accepted an appointment to the board of the Brazos River Authority, having agreed in advance to vote to sell the BRA's lakefront holdings. Assume further that this individual's promise to do so was made in exchange for a promise to be appointed to the board of an even more prestigious or influential state agency. That would be a bribe on someone's part.

Or assume, perhaps, that an individual agreed to temporarily serve on the board of directors of the Brazos River Authority just long enough to vote to sell the BRA's lakefront holdings. In exchange, further assume that the governor of Texas had promised to campaign for you in your subsequent campaign for elected office. That would be a bribe on someone's part.

---

47   In 1989, when the Texas Senate had a debate on a bill to gut state workers' compensation laws, Pilgrim handed out $10,000 checks on the Senate floor. Pilgrim was a supporter of the bill.

Similarly, assume for the sake of argument that an existing board member agreed to withdraw his or her opposition to selling the lakefront holdings in exchange for a juicier appointment from the governor. That would be a bribe on someone's part. Likewise, assume that an individual accepted a position on the board of the BRA, agreeing in advance to support divestiture, based on the promise of a significant bonus, or a significant promotion, or even simply continued employment in his or her private career. That would be a bribe on someone's part.

Besides ruining the political careers of a great many individuals, the Sharpstown stock-fraud scandal resulted in a great many reform laws being passed in 1973. These laws addressed such matters as the bribery statutes and the concept of open meetings. We may be about to find out if those reform measures were sustainable.

Question 3 on the table is whether or not a public servant—elected or appointed—voted to sell the lakefront holdings of the Brazos River Authority in exchange for some benefit.

Bid-Rigging

The River Card's deal to purchase the inhabited shoreline at Possum Kingdom Lake for $50 million resulted from what was supposedly a blind, competitive bid process.

The single most obvious question in all of this is why someone would introduce a middle man into the equation. House Bill 3031 specified exactly what each lot beneath each home had to be sold for. Had there been no middle man in this deal, then the $40 million that went into the River Card's pocket would have gone into the pocket of the BRA. Instead of receiving $50 million for the property, the BRA would have received $90 million.

As we shall see, the River Card was intimately involved in the construction of the request for bids that was issued by the BRA to sell the property. Moreover, he was intimately involved in the crafting of HB 3031, which sanctified his deal.

Why would the Brazos River Authority or the Texas legislature do this?

Question 4 on the table is whether or not the mechanism used to sell the individual lots to the individual leaseholders was simply a legitimate form of bureaucratic and legislative bungling or if it was a fraud perpetrated against the taxpayers of Texas in the form of a rigged bid.

Open Meetings

The image of a smoke-filled chamber where matters of public interest are deliberated by power brokers in secret is a common stereotype of Texas politics. Many would argue that this stereotype has been well earned. In 1993, the Texas legislature once again attempted to remove this stigma by amending Title 5 of the Government Code. Section 551, Chapter 143, states:

> Sec. 551.143. CONSPIRACY TO CIRCUMVENT CHAPTER; OFFENSE; PENALTY. (a) A member or group of members of a governmental body commits an offense if the member or group of members knowingly conspires to circumvent this chapter by meeting in numbers less than a quorum for the purpose of secret deliberations in violation of this chapter.
>
> (b) An offense under Subsection (a) is a misdemeanor punishable by:
>
> (1) a fine of not less than $100 or more than $500;
>
> (2) confinement in the county jail for not less than one month or more than six months; or
>
> (3) both the fine and confinement.

For example, if the governor's office were to conduct a nine-hour meeting with a small, hand-selected group of members of a governmental agency to negotiate the sale of a multimillion-dollar state asset; that would be a crime.

Question 5 on the table is whether or not a state asset worth almost $1 billion was negotiated away behind closed doors for pennies on the dollar.

Cronyism

Cronyism is an ugly term for horse trading that is most often invoked by someone on the losing end of a transaction. Say, for instance, a tied-up goat.

In the state of Texas, cronyism is most easily recognized in appointments that are made by the governor in exchange for political loyalty. During a four-year term, the governor will make about three thousand appointments. Because of his tenure in the governor's mansion, there is not one single state appointee who was not appointed by Governor Rick Perry. After twelve years in office, he is no longer the governor of Texas; he is the CEO of Texas. The final question on the table is this: If one man appoints every nonelected official in a state that is *"Wide Open for Business,"* what could possibly go wrong?

I have heard it said more than once that in order to prove a crime, you must first establish a motive. While I cannot swear that this is correct, it does occur to me that it could prove helpful to reflect on what was motivating the players involved in this deal back in 2009.

Unfortunately, it is impossible to know what was in someone's mind five years ago. However, if you look at the actions of the key players over that time period you *might* gain a glimpse into what their respective motives *might* have been.

1. Governor Rick Perry *might* have wanted to be the president of the United States. He ran for that office in 2012 and went down in flames.
2. Lt. Governor David Dewhurst *might* have wanted to be a US senator. He ran for that office in 2012 and went down in flames, losing to Ted Cruz. He is currently fighting for his political survival.
3. Attorney General Greg Abbott *might* have wanted to be the governor of the state of Texas someday. He is currently on the 2014 ballot for that office.
4. State Senator Glenn Hegar *might* have wanted to be the state comptroller someday. He is currently on the 2014 ballot for that office.
5. State Senator Craig Estes *might* have simply wanted to rebound from the bankruptcy of his family's business.
6. State Representative Jim Keffer *might* have wanted to be the Speaker of the House someday. He campaigned for that office in the fall of 2008 but lost to the current speaker Joe Straus.

7. State Representative Dan Branch *might* have wanted to be the attorney general someday. He is currently on the 2014 ballot for that office.

8. State Representative Brandon Creighton *might* have wanted to seek higher office. In 2013 he announced that he would run for agriculture commissioner but instead is on the 2014 ballot for the state senate.

9. The River Card *might* have wanted to get rich.

10. The bankers staking the River Card *might* have wanted to cash in on his deal.

11. The wealthy leaseholders at Possum Kingdom Lake *might* have wanted to buy the dirt beneath their weekend homes for pennies on the dollar.

Given these *potential* ambitions, it is not hard to see how this group *might* have formed a strategic partnership. Given what was at stake, I became interested in this deal.

To fully understand and appreciate how these strategic partners pulled this off, you will first need to be aware of how they failed on their first attempt. I would suggest to you that the illicit genius of House Bill 3031 in 2009 was born out of the comedic debacle of Senate Bill 1326 in 2007.

I would further suggest to you that your reading of the next few chapters will be enhanced appreciably by a good scotch or a nice glass of wine, depending on your proclivities.[48] Please do not attempt to commit every name, date, or detail to your memory bank. Rather, I would encourage you to treat the balance of *Round I* as pleasure reading. The facts and figures will be duly noted in the footnotes, but the flavor of this tale will be best consumed at your leisure.

I hope that it proves to be worth your while.

---

48 Big word, eh?

Chapter 5

THE JACK OF EASTLAND

It was mentioned earlier that the River Card was holding a suited jack-queen in the pocket when he was taking down the pot. It is time to lift those cards back up and take another peek at the jack.

According to the Texas State Directory, Representative James L. (Jim) Keffer maintained a district office at 1100 East Highway 377 in Granbury during the battle over divestiture. This building was a beautiful Austin-limestone structure and served as the Granbury branch of Southwest Securities, FSB. The adjacent office space at the front of the bank was occupied by Senator Kip Averitt.

In a mass e-mail sent to the party faithful a few years back, the chairman of the Republican Party of Texas, Steve Munisteri, described Representative Jim Keffer in the following fashion:

> "A True Texas Taxpayer Watchdog", State Representative Jim Keffer (R-Eastland) is a conservative family man, small business owner and a lifelong Texas Republican. He is pro-life and pro-property owner/gun owner rights.
>
> Prior to running for the Texas legislature, Jim served as Republican County Chairman for Eastland County. In 1997, he became

the first Republican to ever represent District 60 and has won overwhelming reelections ever since. In his first session, Jim co-authored and passed the "Texas Taxpayer Appraisal Bill of Rights" which created the first-ever cap on property tax appraisals and enabled portability of senior citizen property tax freezes.

Jim and his wife, Leslie, first met at a church summer camp in East Texas. This year, they will be celebrating their 36th wedding anniversary and have 3 grown sons and a granddaughter. Representative Keffer is a graduate of Texas Tech University and is president of a family owned and operated iron foundry business with plants in Eastland and Albany, Texas. As president of EBAA Iron Sales, Inc., Keffer is one of the largest employers in his community. Jim has also given generously with his time in the community. He has served as Deacon and Sunday School Teacher in the first Baptist Church of Eastland, Past President of the Eastland Little League and is active with economic development through his local Chamber of Commerce and in the Texas Association of Business.

Representative Keffer does indeed run the business that his wife's family started. He also serves as a board director for First Financial Bank, Eastland, which was one of the River Card's preferred lenders. And he was also the official author of HB 3031.

Jim Keffer's political career began in obscurity out in the middle of nowhere. His first campaign effort generated a total of $50,692, and his most noteworthy contributors were Mr. and Mrs. Chester R. Upham Jr., who invested $750 in the upstart politician. During his second campaign cycle, which ended in the year 2000, Keffer raised $72,235, although the Upham investment had been reduced to $600. The 2002 cycle saw the Upham support elevated to $3,000, and Keffer's total take that year doubled to $152,996.

Jim Keffer's political and fund-raising fortunes took a significant turn for the better during the 2004 cycle, when he landed a $5,000 donation from a woman who owned a ranch along the Brazos River south of Possum Kingdom Lake. In 2005, Jim Keffer sponsored Senate Bill 1354, which was authored by Senator Craig Estes. This bill was signed into law by Governor Rick Perry on June 17, 2005, and it designated the 113-mile segment of the

Brazos River between Possum Kingdom and Lake Granbury as the John Graves Scenic Waterway.

Named for the famous Texas writer, John Alexander Graves III, the waterway epitomizes the Brazos River, as described in Graves's 1960 book, *Goodbye to a River*. The award-winning book contains a personal and historic account of Graves's journey by canoe down the Brazos River before the building of the current-day reservoirs. By virtue of this designation, this stretch of the Brazos River now enjoys environmental protection and special oversight by the Brazos River Authority.

During the following campaign cycle that ended in 2006, this same rancher expressed her appreciation for Keffer's efforts to protect her environment by contributing $20,000 to his coffers. This was his largest single contribution to date and he was now a made-man. His total take that season was $402,330, which more than doubled the $183,173 that he had raised in 2004.

The breadth of our lady rancher's appreciation was not limited to Jim Keffer. During the 2006 season, she rewarded Governor Rick Perry with two contributions totaling $110,000; Lieutenant Governor David Dewhurst with four contributions, totaling $61,000; Senator Craig Estes with two contributions, totaling $50,000; Attorney General Greg Abbott with two contributions, totaling $35,000; House Speaker Tom Craddick with two contributions, totaling $30,000; and Senator Kim Brimer with two contributions, totaling a paltry $15,000.

All told, her thank-you notes totaled $356,000. Yes indeed, a polite Texan knows how to say thank-you, even the ones who are not actually from Texas.

During the previous election cycle, our fair lady had contributed a total of $80,000 to this same group of environmental stalwarts. Since I have seen this lady's lawyers in action, I will be the last man alive to suggest that this was a merit raise or a political payoff. Her criminal lawyer can make a DWI charge disappear faster than a tied-up goat's dignity. If you consider that to be a cowardly stance, then you can kiss my ass. If you can convince anyone with a lick of common sense that this was anything other than a political payoff, then I will kiss your ass.

Wealthy ranchers in Texas are not uncommon, nor are wealthy female ranchers who control their own purse strings. What is unique about this particular female rancher who owned the Rocking W Ranch is that her last name is Walton, and her father's first name was Sam. Her mother's name was Helen. Alice Louise Walton was born on October 7, 1949, and she is an heiress to the Walmart fortune. She is now considered to be one of the richest women in the world, according to *Forbes* magazine, with a net worth that exceeds $21 billion.

Representative Jim Keffer, Senator Craig Estes, and the leadership of the Republican Party in Texas had landed a whale. Not only was Jim Keffer now a made-man, but a repeatable business model had been established. Repurposing the natural resources of the state of Texas for the benefit of wealthy individuals had been proven politically expedient and financially lucrative. If this business model was executed properly through the legislative process, then no one could complain. The political sale of the state treasures of Texas was officially underway.

While Representative Jim Keffer was ensuring that any trash or debris that accumulated along the river shore of Alice Walton's ranch would be cleaned up by the Brazos River Authority, he was also aware of the fact that something called the Staubach Report was looming. His legislative response was to issue the following resolution during the same Seventy-Ninth Legislative Session.[49]

H.R. No. 2194

RESOLUTION

WHEREAS, The Brazos River Authority was created by the Texas Legislature in Chapter 221, Water Code; and

WHEREAS, The leaseholders and residents of the Possum Kingdom Community have invested heavily in improvements to those parcels of land and development of the Possum Kingdom Community in general; and

WHEREAS, The unencumbered, underdeveloped land surrounding Possum Kingdom Lake adds value to the area property today and preserves the natural beauty of Possum Kingdom Lake for future generations; now, therefore, be it

---

49 Jim Keffer, "House Resolution 2194," Texas Legislature, June 1, 2005, accessed March 10, 2010. http://www.legis.state.tx.us/BillLookup/History.aspx?LegSess=79R&Bill=HR2194.

RESOLVED, That the House of Representatives of the 79th Texas Legislature hereby direct the Brazos River Authority to work with the leaseholders and residents of Possum Kingdom Lake Community on the future direction of the area; and, be it further

RESOLVED, That the Brazos River Authority not engage in divestiture of real property prior to the 80th Legislative Session and that legislators have an opportunity for input into this complex and important activity; and, be it further

RESOLVED, That an official copy of this resolution be forwarded to the chair of the Brazos River Authority as an expression of the sentiment of the Texas House of Representatives.

Keffer of Eastland

Speaker of the House

I certify that H.R. No. 2194 was adopted by the House on May 27, 2005, by a non-record vote.

Chief Clerk of the House

House Resolution No. 2194 provided the first hint that certain members of the Texas Legislature intended to determine the outcome of the investments that the weekenders had made at Possum Kingdom Lake. Given that the board of the Brazos River Authority would soon ignore this nonbinding resolution, it was also the first hint that those board members could not take a hint.

There will be substantially more color provided on both Jim Keffer and Alice Walton as we progress, but for the time being, we need to try to figure out how this all got started. To accomplish that, we will need to take a stroll down memory lane.

Chapter 6

THE STAUBACH REPORT

Following a legendary career as the quarterback of the Dallas Cowboys, Roger Staubach formed a real estate advisory firm in 1977 that bore his name. The Staubach Company is recognized as a global market leader, and the firm's reputation for integrity is commensurate with the reputation of the man himself.

In 2004, the Brazos River Authority commissioned the Staubach Company to perform a study of the Authority's strategic options. On April 11, 2006, the Staubach Company presented the results of their multiphase, multiyear analysis. The introduction of the Staubach Report's Phase III analysis provides a crystal-clear synopsis of the situation that set this scheme in motion.

Refill your drink, and then read on.

> Land surrounding recreational lakes has significantly increased in both popularity and value over the past several decades. As a result of the increased values of land surrounding lakes and waterways, there is a significant amount of change taking place in and around these bodies of water. This is the case across the United States as

well as in Texas. It is particularly true for Possum Kingdom Lake, which is managed by the Brazos River Authority.

In 1928, The Brazos River Authority, originally the Brazos River Conservation and Reclamation District, was created by the State of Texas to "conserve, control and utilize to beneficial service the storm and flood waters of the Brazos River and its tributary streams."

Due, in large part, to major flooding in the area in the first half of the 20th Century, a dam on the Brazos River in northwest Palo Pinto County was proposed in the 1930s and construction began in 1938. This was the first major project undertaken by the new Conservation District, and was completed under the District's first Master Plan.

Morris Sheppard Dam was completed in 1941, and Lake Possum Kingdom was created. The Brazos River Authority has managed the Dam, Lake and much of the surrounding property since that time as part of its mandate.

Originally, Possum Kingdom Lake (PKL) was far from any major city. As the DFW Metroplex has grown in the past several decades, both in geographical size and population, PKL has become a major destination and recreation lake for residents of the area. Additionally, the construction of resorts and communities surrounding the lake has added to the commercial capacity and appeal of the lake and its surroundings.

With the increase in popularity has come a corresponding increase in the value of land surrounding the lake. The BRA's management practices at PKL have not always kept up with the times. In the late 1990s, the BRA contracted the Tennessee Valley Authority (TVA), one of the nation's premier water authorities and land managers, to undertake a strategic study of PKL and surrounding BRA lands.

The TVA report was completed in 2000 and introduced several major recommendations. Among these were recommendations to:

- Increase cottage leases to fair market values,

- Implement a comprehensive land information system,

- Create a financial atmosphere that leads to desired development,

- BRA must be very diligent in its planning with regard to siting, solid waste and wastewater, and lake access arrangements in order to protect the scenic and environmental qualities that make it attractive for the various uses mentioned above,

- BRA should begin to move toward full cost recovery on its solid waste operations,

- Road construction and maintenance is another function that BRA must continue, especially since most of the activity is on BRA property. The cost of this function should be considered when setting fees.

The TVA noted "In summary, there is no real prospect that the counties can or will assume in the near future any of the community service functions that BRA currently has. Therefore, we recommend that BRA recognize these functions as a cost of providing quality facilities and experiences to its lessees and to the general public."

The BRA instituted some of the recommended steps, most notably a plan to increase lease rates to reflect fair market value. With severe pressure from lessees and politicians, the BRA changed its policies a number of times. This resulted in confusion and mistrust among all parties.

While the BRA situation at PKL continued in a state of flux, development surrounding the lake on non-BRA lands, and, to some extent, on BRA lands, was ongoing. Much of this development was taking advantage of the void in BRA plans. Without any long-term BRA plan in place, these commercial offerings sought to lock up new lake residents and access to the lake.

The increased development and demands on the BRA for land, access and water only served to bring notice that there was even more of a need for a master plan. In order to keep up with the growth at PKL, the BRA enlisted The Staubach Company to undertake a complete Strategic Study of the situation at PKL and make recommendations as to how to best manage its assets.

In Phase I of its review, The Staubach Company (TSC) performed a review of the current situation and practices at PKL. Next, in Phase II, TSC reviewed other properties with similar characteristics to those at PKL. TSC then benchmarked the BRA's operations and practices against these other properties and practices to help determine where BRA and PKL stack up.

The next step in this process is Phase III, which is contained in this report. In this report, TSC looks at options for the BRA land and its management practices. The financial, environmental and market impacts were considered among other important issues for each option. Finally, taking all the factors into consideration, TSC makes a number of recommendations as to what course of action the BRA should take.[50]

Were it not for the Possum Kingdom Lake Association's website, it would be difficult to fully understand what the Staubach Report meant by "severe pressure from lessees and politicians." It would also be difficult to appreciate the PKLA's ability to wield the political power necessary to achieve their desired outcome.

Through their meeting minutes and newsletters, the PKLA went to great lengths to document what they wanted and how they intended to get it. When the PKLA leadership saw the following recommendations of the Staubach Report reduced to writing in April 2006, the table was set for a winner-take-all game of poker.

Recommendations Summary:

Residential Leases

The BRA is currently landlord to approximately 1,600 residential leases surrounding PKL, comprising the most valuable property which the BRA owns—the shoreline. The past actions of the BRA and the lessees have created an environment of confused perceptions, mistrust and inequality. TSC thoroughly considered the intentions and results of these past actions in consolidating these recommendations.

The following recommendations can bring stability and equality to the current residential lease environment at PK by allowing the BRA to gain a reasonable return on its assets while implementing a fair and consistent set of lease terms for the tenants.

1: Implement new lease document

50 The Staubach Company, "Phase III Report—Introduction," April 11, 2006, accessed May 14, 2011. http://www.brazos.org/generalPdf/Staubach_PIII_Section1.pdf.

Implement a new lease form which contains updated and clearly defined terms and conditions based on current industry practices. (See Exhibits—Summary Key BRA Lease Provisions)

2: Modify rental rate methodology

Remove current cap on lease rates—this allows the rental methodology to continue on a gradual increase to market based lease rates (from 3% to 6% over 20 years) and eliminates the current inequality;

Market Value—Tie lease rates directly to the fair market value of the land derived by licensed MAI1 real estate appraisers, not on the current ambiguous and inconsistent county assessor values;

Incentive for Lessees—Give current lessees an option to enter into a new long term lease at a substantially reduced rate. The proposed incentive equates to an initial rental rate based on 35% of fair market value and increases to 60% over a 30 year term. Offer this incentive for a limited term (12–24 months).

3: Increase new residential terms of 30 years minimum and 50 years maximum.

Increase minimum lease terms to 30 years and no more than 50 years. A minimum 30 year term enables a lessee to obtain a competitive market rate mortgage for the improvements.

4: Standardize lake use policies for all lake users

Apply lake use policies consistently to all lake users. Adjust specific policies to reflect, at minimum, the actual cost of services:

Lake water usage—Charge all lake users equally. The BRA currently waives the $37.10 per year charge to lessees. Increase water fee to $50.00 ($4.17 per month). Estimate of additional revenue: $58,665.

Boat docks—Charged all dock owners equally. The BRA currently waives the $.10 per square foot annual charge for residential docks to lessees. Increase this fee to $0.20 per square foot per year. This equates to an average of $180 per year ($15 per month) for a 900 square foot dock. Estimated additional revenue: $198,000.

Boat user fees—Charge all watercraft owners equally. The BRA currently waives the $50 per year watercraft fee for lessees. Estimated additional revenue: $79,000.

Road Maintenance—Implement a program to make road maintenance self-sustaining. Conduct a complete survey of the BRA roads and utilize the GIS capabilities of the BRA to allocate road maintenance expenses directly to those properties which receive the benefit.

Much of the leased property utilizes BRA maintained roads as access. In a market based rental methodology, any access issues would be considered by an appraiser, and therefore, in the ultimate market value of the property and in the resulting calculated rent. Road maintenance would be a part of the rent. This is not the case under the current methodology where such characteristics are not considered in the valuation. Without this consideration, the costs associated with the roads should be allocated on a pro-rata basis, according to use. Properties which have no access issues clearly would not receive associated assessments. Those properties on roads which do require substantial maintenance should be assessed associated costs.

5: Lease assignments

Do not allow unrestricted transfers of leasehold interests. Require that buyers of leasehold estates be subject to market rate based rents. This eliminates the current practice of allowing lessees to capture the appreciation on BRA lakefront property upon a sale. Grant the incentive to any new leasehold purchaser who buys within the extended 12–24 month period of time.

This allows a current lessee to sell near current prices should they decide to exit the market.

6: Require new leases rather than automatic options to renew

Require new leases at market rates upon expiration of a lease, rather than granting automatic extensions. This provides flexibility in management of the assets and allows for implementation of new forms, policies and procedures.

7: Implement an inspection program

Implement a program for the periodic inspection of each leasehold estate to insure compliance to lease restrictions and the shoreline management guide. Require a current inspection for the issuance of each permit (construction, etc.).

8: Implement mandatory appraisals

In conjunction with the portfolio management strategy, require a current appraisal on each leasehold property at the time any new lease is executed.[51]

While none of these recommendations were well received by the weekenders, the recommendations related to tying rental rates to fair market value were the game changers. Beyond the scenic beauty of the landscape, the primary attraction of Possum Kingdom Lake was the fact that you were paying virtually nothing to enjoy it. Without a doubt, these people had grown accustomed to having the taxpayers of Texas subsidize their weekend lifestyles. Introducing the practice of fair market appraisals would eliminate the free ride that they had enjoyed for generations.

On May 22, 2006, the BRA board of directors met to, among other things, review the recommendations of the Staubach Report and take action on those recommendations. At about one hour into the discussion, CEO Phil Ford read a letter faxed from Senator Craig Estes that was addressed to Mr. Steve Pena, Mr. Wade Gear, and Mr. Phil Ford. It was dated May 18, 2006.

> To: Mr. Steve Pena
>
> Mr. Wade Gear
>
> Mr. Phil Ford
>
> From: Senator Craig Estes
>
> Date: May 18, 2006
>
> RE: Possum Kingdom Lake Leaseholders
>
> My staff and I have been in contact with some businessmen from the Dallas area who are leaseholders at Possum Kingdom Lake. I, like you, have had numerous conversations over the past few years about the issues surrounding the future of leases on and around Possum Kingdom Lake. These gentlemen have offered to me, as I know they will you, a refreshing positive approach to this situation. These stakeholders are Lance Byrd, Pat McLochlin, Jim Shields, and Jay Turner.

---

51   The Staubach Company, "Phase III Report—Recommendations Summary," April 11, 2006, accessed May 14, 2011, http://www.brazos.org/generalPdf/Staubach_PIII_Section8.pdf.

Like many leaseholders at Possum Kingdom, these gentlemen oppose the adoption of the Staubach Report as currently under consideration by the BRA Board of Directors. Unlike much of what we've heard, their approach to their disagreement is not based on emotions or the familiar defense of status quo. They realize that lease rates should increase, for example, but with reason and predictability. They seek to be a resource in the development of a permanent solution to the BRA/PK issue that is beneficial to all concerned parties both now and in the future.

These stakeholders have convinced me that they should be a part of a positive, solution-seeking process in which their suggestions for meeting BRA's needs are considered and a consensual solution is reached. They have expressed to me a concern that all previous venues of interaction have put them in a reactionary position regarding the proposed plans, and they would like an opportunity to legitimately counter-off. More importantly, they believe that they have something positive to add to the discourse surrounding the Possum Kingdom Lake issues that will raise the level of the discussion. I agree.

For these reasons I ask that you three gentlemen hold a meeting with these gentlemen in the very near future. I ask that you have a conversation in which you share the long-term goals, plans, and needs of the BRA. In turn, I ask that you listen to the concerns and suggestions of these leaseholders.

I have asked these gentlemen to refrain from engaging in any external influence in the working of the BRA on this issue. This request was predicated and contingent upon the assumption that no action on The Staubach Company report will be taken by the BRA prior to the meeting with them I am requesting.

It is with great optimism that I make the request for your conversation with these leaseholders. I look forward to seeing your dates of availability to meet with them. Please inform me of those potential dates, times, and locations before the close of business on May 26, 2006. I also look forward to hearing of the positive outcome of these meetings, as I believe they will be so.

The BRA and the affected leaseholders are long-time partners. Each needs the other to be healthy. It is my hope that you seven gentlemen, in the absence of outside interference, might develop a method of ensuring the future well-being of all parties.

Thank you for your tireless efforts in pursuing what is best for all.[52]

Following that, Phil Ford read a second letter from State Representative Phil King, who represented District 61. King's letter contained a similar request for postponing action.

May 18, 2006

Mr. Phillip J. Ford
General Manager/CEO
Brazos River Authority
P.O. Box 7555
Waco, TX 76714-7555

Dear Mr. Ford:

I have recently received several calls from concerned constituents that own property at Possum Kingdom Lake. They have called to my attention that the Brazos River Authority Board is going to be having a meeting to possibly vote on the recommendations that the Staubach Company made in regard to property surrounding the lake on May 22nd.

Upon review of these recommendations it is clear that if the BRA does choose to adopt them, there will be some major fiscal implications to property owners at Possum Kingdom Lake. Because of the serious nature of these implications, it is my hope that the BRA board will choose to postpone the vote on this matter for at least 60 days in order to give the property owners that will potentially be affected more time to study how they will be impacted.

I appreciate your consideration in this matter and look forward to your prompt response.

Sincerely,

Phil King

---

52   Phil Ford, "Special Board Meeting—Agenda Item 10," Brazos River Authority Board of Directors Audio Meetings Minutes, 60:00, May 22, 2006, accessed November 18, 2010. http://brazos.org/board_audio/05222006_Special_PK_BRD10.mp3.

Cc: The Honorable Greg Abbott, Attorney General of Texas[53]

Why would Representative Phil King copy the attorney general of Texas? We will get to that later.

The directors of the BRA's board were incredulous. One member stated that it was obvious that the politicians were attempting to take the matter out of the hands of the board. Another asked why the businessmen from Dallas had not previously submitted their "positive suggestions" to the BRA during the public comment process. Yet another stated that this was simply another tactic to delay the introduction of market-based rental policies.

Shortly after these letters were read, the board recessed for lunch. When they reconvened, a vote was taken to consider the recommendations of the Staubach Report. After thirty minutes of discussion, a motion was made to adopt market-oriented rental rates. When the board was polled, the result was almost unanimous at 20 to 1. The only *No* vote came from Director Martha Stovall Martin, who, along with her husband, David, lived on roughly 1.4 acres of lakefront property that they were leasing from the Brazos River Authority. In 2008, that property carried an assessed value of $216,500.

Later that evening, the Brazos River Authority issued the following press release:

FOR IMMEDIATE RELEASE

CONTACT: Judi Pierce

Public Information Officer

(254) 761-3103

THE BRAZOS RIVER AUTHORITY BOARD APPROVES LONGER LEASE TERMS AND RATE INCENTIVES FOR POSSUM KINGDOM LAKE LESSEES

May 22, 2006—Waco, Texas—The Brazos River Authority (BRA) Board of Directors voted today to approve a property management plan and lease rate methodology for cottage site leases at Possum Kingdom Lake. At a specially called meeting

---

53   Phil Ford, "Special Board Meeting—Agenda Item 10," Brazos River Authority Board of Directors Audio Meetings Minutes, 60:00, May 22, 2006, accessed November 18, 2010. http://brazos.org/board_audio/05222006_Special_PK_BRD10.mp3.

at the BRA's Central Offices in Waco, the Board of Directors approved the plan that provides for a gradual increase in lease rates over time while offering discounts to current lessees who choose to sign a new lease form.

Based on the results of studies conducted by the Staubach Company and the Tennessee Valley Authority (TVA), the staff recommended a methodology that will continue to be based on appraisal district values. The Board chose not to adopt an approach based on actual market values. An increase to six percent of appraised values will be implemented in 5-year increments over a 20 year period. A new provision allows current lessees that choose to sign a newly revised lease form to take advantage of an attractive incentive program, and also offers a 30–50-year lease term, making bank financing easier to obtain.

"Our hope was to have a final vote on the management plan and lease rate methodology that is fair and equitable—we believe we have achieved those results," said Steve Pena, BRA Board presiding officer. "The due diligence has lasted for several years and we believe the final product is a compromise that will balance the needs of the lessees with that of the Authority."

The new lease rate methodology will be implemented beginning January 1, 2008 and will be based on 2007 appraisal district values. The Authority staff has been directed to begin work on recommendations for a discounted lease rate for those lessees' 65-years of age and older who are eligible for homestead rights on their leased site.

The Board also approved Boating Capacity Studies for Lakes Possum Kingdom and Granbury as well as a continued moratorium on cut-through canals at Lake Granbury. These measures were approved in keeping with the Board's continued efforts to protect the environment while preserving and enhancing the quality of available local water resources.[54]

---

54 Judi Pierce, "The Brazos River Authority Board Approves Longer Lease Terms and Rate Incentives for Possum Kingdom Lake Lessees," Brazos River Authority, April 27, 2007, accessed February 1, 2014. http://www.brazos.org/newsPdf/PKLeaseRaterelease-DRAFT31.pdf.

The game was now on, and those members of the Brazos River Authority's board who truly wanted to protect the interests of the taxpayers of Texas would be put to the test. To make sure that the battle lines were clearly drawn, the Possum Kingdom Community Advisory Panel had sent the following resolution to the BRA board of directors one month earlier, in anticipation of the release of the Staubach Report.

Resolution to Brazos River Authority passed by the BRA Community Advisory Panel

The CAP members present at the meeting approved by a unanimous vote the following resolution:

The Possum Kingdom Community Advisory Panel (CAP) an entity created by the Board of Directors (BOD) of the Brazos River Authority to receive and communicate information regarding the Authority's management and administration of Possum Kingdom Lake hereby recommends to the Possum Kingdom Committee the following resolution at its April 11, 2006 meeting:

BE IT RESOLVED that the Community Advisory Panel hereby recommends to the Brazos River Authority dissolution of the Community Advisory Panel, as evidenced by a majority vote wherein Community Advisory Panel members resigned their positions; and

BE IT FURTHER RESOLVED that the Community Advisory Panel recommends to the Brazos River Authority continuation of efforts in public communication with Possum Kingdom residents through the Possum Kingdom Lake Association.[55]

The game was also on now for those leaseholders who had invested large sums of money in their weekend homes at Possum Kingdom Lake. While the resolution adopted on May 26, 2006, stopped short of introducing fair market appraisals into the equation, the result of an increase in rental rates would be an overnight decrease in the value of their investments. It was time to go to Austin and do some business.

---

55   "Community Advisory Panel Meeting," Possum Kingdom Lake Association, June 23, 2007, accessed December 12, 2010. http://www.pklakeassn.org/BRACAP_1_23_06.html.

The task would not be simple. The only way for the wealthy weekenders to insulate themselves from rising rental rates was to buy the property beneath their weekend homes. The only way to protect their investments was to do so at a deep discount. Given that there was no shortage of laws on the books designed to prevent this from happening, the desired result would require a concerted effort on the part of many. Those laws included:

1. The Texas Local Government Code, Chapter 272;[56]
2. The Texas Water Code, Section 49.226;[57]
3. The Texas Special District Local Laws Code, Section 8502.013;[58] and
4. The Texas State Constitution, Article III, Section 52.[59]

We are going to need more lawyers.

---

56 Texas Local Government Code, Chapter 272, http://www.statutes.legis.state.tx.us/Docs/LG/htm/LG.272.htm.

57 Texas Water Code, Section 49.226, http://www.statutes.legis.state.tx.us/Docs/WA/htm/WA.49.htm#49.226.

58 Texas Special District Local Laws Code, Section 8502.013, http://www.statutes.legis.state.tx.us/Docs/SD/htm/SD.8502.htm#8502.013.

59 Texas State Constitution, Article III, Section 52, http://www.statutes.legis.state.tx.us/Docs/CN/htm/CN.3.htm#3.52.

Chapter 7

THE AUSTIN MEETING

The Texas legislature is only in session for five out of every twenty-four months in the odd-numbered years. The old joke in Texas is that the state constitution provides for this to limit the damage that the legislature can do. Fortunately for the PKLA and the PKLPA, the Eightieth Legislative Session of 2007 opened seven months after the introduction of the Staubach Report. When that session started, they were ready to do their business—or so they thought.

On March 7, 2007, Senator Craig Estes filed Senate Bill 1326, which was designed to force the Brazos River Authority to sell its lakefront lots to the individual lessees of those lots. Two weeks later, on Tuesday, March 20, a nine-hour meeting was held in Austin to negotiate the terms and conditions of the forced sale.

The fastest way to turn *The Tale of the River Card* into a libel suit against yours truly would be for me to attempt to explain what happened during that meeting. So to avoid that outcome, I will let those who were involved in the meeting do it for me.

Three days after this all-important meeting in Austin, the General Manager/CEO of the Brazos River Authority, Mr. Phil Ford, sent what might be the shortest status report of all time to the governor's office.

From: Phil Ford

Sent: Friday, March 23, 2007 9:06 AM

To: Kenneth Anderson; Phil Wilson; Steve Pena

Cc: dpearson@hillcopartners.com

Subject: FW: Work continues on BRA land sale bills

Attachments: Work continues on BRA land sale bills.doc

fyi[60]

That one acronym in the e-mail spoke volumes. The attachment to his e-mail was the text of a newspaper article that had come out that morning in the *Lake Country Sun*. That article provided an accounting of the meeting and read as follows:

Work Continues on BRA Land Sale Bills

Michael Matthews

news@lakecountrysun.com

March 23, 2007

An important meeting was held Tuesday in a Senate conference room at the Texas Capitol pertaining to legislation filed March 7 that would allow lessees of Brazos River Authority properties at Possum Kingdom Lake to purchase their leased land.

If Senate Bill 1326, by Sen. Craig Estes, R-Wichita Falls, and House Bill 2923, by Rep. Jim Keffer, R-Eastland, are enacted, they would circumvent certain state restrictions and regulations impeding such a divestiture, and compel the authority to begin accepting applications to purchase residential lots from lessees within 90 days of passage.

Tuesday's meeting was instigated by Estes as a workshop for the primary parties to analyze provisions of the legislation and to work out any differences or disagreements.

---

60   Phil Ford, "Re: Work Continues on BRA Land Sale Bills," e-mail message to Kenneth Anderson, Phil Wilson, March 23, 2007, accessed June 13, 2013.

Participants included representatives of the BRA, Gov. Rick Perry's office, the Possum Kingdom Lake Preservation Association and Possum Kingdom Lake Association, as well as the senator and representative and members of their staffs.

According to Monte and Carolyn Land, who represented the PKLA, approximately 30 people crowded a fairly chaotic morning session, then about 10 were invited to participate in a much more productive afternoon session that lasted several hours.

Lewis Simmons, chief of staff for Estes, moderated Tuesday's meeting and reported Wednesday that compromises were reached on all important matters of contention, such as an appraisal methodology.

Simmons said he expected the legislation to move forward with cooperation from all the participants.

"It was a very good meeting," Simmons said Wednesday. "Very productive. The lessees at PK Lake should be happy to know that we preserved the integrity of the bill."

"I think it's going to happen," PKLA's Carolyn Land said of divestiture. "I think we've got a shot at getting it passed."

Simmons explained a new draft will direct that appraisals of land value, the first of which must be procured and paid for by lessees applying to purchase the land, would be based on "fair market value of the land." The wording of the legislation filed read, "fair market value of the interest being acquired."

The original legislation designated that the BRA, rather than the lessee, hire and pay the first appraiser.

The appraisal would be part of an application package, and if the BRA disputes the appraised value, the authority could pay for a second opinion. The cost of a third appraisal, needed only if two differing appraisals could not be reconciled, would be shared.

Other small corrections were agreed upon, and a new draft of the legislation is currently being written. Carolyn Land said no other change agreed upon was considered major.

The language compromise does not bother attorney Robert Aldrich, representing PKLPA, but he insists the laws regarding property appraisal are specific and opposed to what the authority wants to do, which is to have the land appraised as though it were already in private hands, though the land has been encumbered by lease agreements for years.

"[The BRA] is still fighting this day by day," Aldrich said Wednesday. "The law says how to do it, but the BRA doesn't want to follow the law. They want a windfall. Yesterday was all about the BRA's continued attempt to have an invalid appraisal methodology used."

Wednesday morning, BRA Public Information Officer Judi Pierce said, "There's really nothing much to comment about until we see the next draft."

Carolyn and Monte Land noted the representatives from Perry's office, Ken Anderson, Phil Wilson and Cody Shorter, were actively involved in the process all day Tuesday. "Absolutely," Simmons concurred. "Their leadership was invaluable. The governor has supported this since day one. He wants the people at PK to be able to own their properties if they wish. And we wanted to be assured we had his support. Everyone was in a cooperative spirit."

Aldrich continues to temper his enthusiasm. "The BRA is not cooperating one iota," he asserted. "But I do think we'll get it done. It's just not going to be easy."

After revisions are made and a draft submitted to negotiating parties, probably by next week, the Senate version will move to the Natural Resources Committee, of which Estes is vice chairman.

Monte Land, PKLA president, said that Estes and Keffer deserve enormous credit for recognizing the difficulties of the people at PK Lake in dealing with the BRA and working toward a solution.

"We don't thank them enough," Land said.

Letters of appreciation may be sent to:

Sen. Craig Estes
P.O. Box 12068
Capitol Station
Austin, TX 78711

Rep. Jim Keffer
P.O. Box 2910
Austin, TX 78768[61]

---

61 Phil Ford, "Re: Work Continues on BRA Land Sale Bills," e-mail message to Kenneth Anderson, Phil Wilson, March 23, 2007, accessed June 13, 2013.

Did you notice that the author of this story was someone named Michael Matthews, not Mark Engebretson?

For some reason, Phil Ford felt compelled to inform the governor's office that the local bait-shop tabloid was covering the story and illuminating the fact that the governor's top lieutenants were identified as key players in the forced divestiture. Ford also pointed out that the journalist who wrote the story was aware that there were laws on the books intended to prevent a sale of this nature from happening.

That following Monday, March 26, 2007, the Brazos River Authority held a special board meeting to discuss Senate Bill 1326. BRA general manager, Phil Ford, opened the dialogue by providing his objectives for the meeting. He then asked Board Director Wade Gear who had attended the entirety of the nine-hour meeting in Austin to provide a recounting of the affair.

> Um, it was a long day. It was a, like I said, it was a mediation-style meeting. There were meetings going on and submeetings going on and people talking in corners and in hallways and it was, uh, it was a mind-draining day. There were multiple occasions where I felt that I was being placed in the position to speak for the board in which on multiple occasions I clearly stated that I represented one board member's opinion. I could not and would not speak for the board.
>
> I told them that the only thing that I know is that in the past, the board has acted, in my opinion, conservatively and compassionately. That we are concerned about people who are on fixed incomes and those folks that have some limited capabilities at the lake, so to speak. The main gist of the day, and you'll see it later, is the appraisal approach which the PKLPA, and the PKLA are indicating they believe to be fair and just. As a matter of fact they kept spitting out that it was law.
>
> Uh, Mr. Staley was the first to speak and told Phil before the meeting started that within the first five minutes, we would know how the meeting was going to go all day and within the first five minutes, you know, there was a bomb went off. Um, I don't tend to agree with Mr. Staley. I'm certainly not an attorney. Uh, if we've been breaking the law for sixty-five years, I would have assumed somebody would have stepped up to the plate and sued us. Maybe that time is coming. I don't know.

There were several requests that I made in the meeting of Mr. Aldrich to provide us with the documentation, the studies, and the research, that these groups have done that countermands the TVA and the Staubach study. Because they repeatedly stated that those studies were flawed. I never got a straight answer.

One of the issues in regards to the fair market value approach is that because the lease is an encumbrance on the land, it affects the value of that land because at closing, there's merger. Meaning the lease merges with the fee simple title. And personally, I think it's double-dipping. I don't like it. I don't support it.

I stated that the BRA would be comfortable with language and only with language that stated the fair market value was to be determined by the unencumbered fee simple estate.

Um, and at which point Mr. Turner quickly said, "Well, that's a deal killer. This meeting is over."

The point I tried to make to them was that fair market includes a willing buyer and a willing seller. We are not a willing seller. We are being forced to sell, and at some point we need to say we are not going to sell it, and we will take the steps necessary not to sell it at this approach.

Personally, I agree with Jay. The language that is in the bill now for my position is a deal killer.

Mr. Staley just stood up and talked about greed. I find that a bit humorous. The chairman of the PKLPA had a home at Possum Kingdom. And one of the issues that we discussed in the meeting, Mr. Aldrich clearly stated to me that he felt the Palo Pinto appraisal district was way out of whack and that their values were overstated.

So I asked Phil to help me with some homework. Now this lot was sold in 2002 before the 2003 assessment came out in March. The 2002 assessment was $439,980. Yet the asking price for this home was $750,000. So clearly someone has put money in their pocket, and it did not go into the pocket of the BRA. So when we talk about greed, maybe we need to spread that around a bit.

I don't believe anyone in this room, because they're all current residents; it applies to them. But there is a large group of people that have sold their homes at fair market value of the unencumbered interest and have left Possum Kingdom. And they have left Possum Kingdom in the position that it is in. I've got some other research coming on some other sales comps so we will be able to look at that.

It was a very frustrating day. It was a very frustrating day, and at the end of the day I was asked specifically if I could live with the language that was in the, that was written "the fair market value of the land."

I said I didn't know. I said I needed to think about it, and I needed to reflect on it. And I went home and I spent a very sleepless night, and I reflected, and I cannot live with that language in the bill. It's a deal killer for me.

This greed issue needs to be nipped in the bud, and, uh, I think there are a lot of people at the lake that don't understand the tactic that they are trying to use with this appraisal approach. And I believe that there was, and I've talked to them, that they felt like they were ready to pay the fair market value of land as they understood it, which was the unencumbered approach. So this is a huge hurdle for us to still get over.

Uh, the other issue that I really have a problem with is the fact the original bill stated—I believe it was the original, I've looked at so many versions—uh, stated that you had to be a leaseholder as of January 1, 2007. That's now changed and as long as you're a leaseholder at the time this bill passes, you are, uh, you are eligible to purchase.

What this does, in my opinion, is it creates a serious inequity because if someone bought a home up there today under their value approach, they would have equity at the time of their closing. They could buy it on a Monday for $100,000 and sell it on Tuesday for $125,000 or whatever.

The other problem I had with it is the fact that if we have a PK resident that's had a lease for thirty years and their lease is up in two years, and their neighbor, same lot, same everything, has a thirty-year lease; the gentleman with the thirty-year lease will pay less for his land than the gentleman with two years remaining. And to me, that rewards the folks that have moved out there in the last five to ten years. And that doesn't sit well with me. Um, so those are two issues that I am real concerned with.

The third and other issue that we really didn't discuss in this meeting—quite frankly, I think everyone was so brain dead at the end of the day; I mean, wouldn't you agree, Martha? I mean we were all walking around like zombies. Um, we didn't discuss the buffer zone. And the philosophy is that they would like a non-exclusive easement if FERC will allow that. They don't want to pay an appurtenant lease.

And let me give you my philosophy on that. I just ran some rough numbers and I assumed 1,500 because I don't know how many people are going to buy. I assumed everyone was going to buy, so I took 1,579. And if everybody had 125 feet of lake frontage at 25 feet deep, and you paid fair market value at 6 percent, we would be leaving over a million dollars a year on the table. And I really think that number is higher. I was trying to be conservative. But not knowing, some people's lots are narrow and deep and some are wide and shallow, there's a lot of variables on that, but that's a lot of money. We have a sixty-five-year history that indicates that that land has value, and now they want it for free. I don't understand that.

Um, and I'm not sure about the constitutionality of it; in that we cannot lend our credit, allowing them to use it. And taking away funds from our downstream customers is a little bit concerning.

And I asked Phil, I said how many people does our system rate affect? And he gave me the estimated municipal population impacted by our system rates is 1,130,000 and some change. Um, that's a lot. There are people downstream that I don't think can be expected to pick up the tab for people's second homes. And I cannot support anything with my senator or my state rep if it doesn't say fair market value of the unencumbered fee simple estate. And, uh, that pretty much sums up the meeting. It was eight and a half hours and eight minutes, so ...

Uh, there was some emotion; there were some tempers; there was a lot of frustration. The governor's office was very helpful in trying to keep a lid on everything and trying to work out workable solutions. But at the end of the day, I felt like we were negotiating away a state asset. And really I did not sleep well that night.[62]

BRA Board Chairman Steve Pena then asked Martha Stovall Martin to share her assessment of the meeting. As a subtle reminder, Director

---

62 Wade Gear, "Special Board Meeting—Agenda Items 5–6," Brazos River Authority Board of Directors Audio Meetings Minutes, 5:30, March 26, 2007, accessed November 18, 2010. http://brazos.org/board_audio/03262007_1SPL2.mp3.

Martin was the only BRA board member to vote against tying the rental rates to fair market value in response to the Staubach Report. She was also the only board member who lived on 1.4 acres of lakefront property at Possum Kingdom Lake. In 2012, after the River Card's deal was done, she and her husband, David, built a new house on the property, valued at roughly $600,000. This brought the total assessed value of their homestead to a tidy $1.1 million.

In her Southern-belle voice, Martha Martin described her observations of the nine-hour meeting as follows:

> Well, true. It was a really interesting day. I've never been a part of negotiations quite like that. But you know, I really thought at the end of the day there had been agreements reached that, and you know I wasn't in there the whole time, that seemed to be acceptable on both sides. So I was a little surprised, you know, just the next day, but you know maybe I didn't hear, you know, your discussions, that you weren't, you know, 100 percent set on, or brain dead, or something.
>
> Um, I hope we can keep working together to negotiate this deal because it affects a lot of people, and I think it can be done. I really hope we can kind of continue on trying to work this out.[63]

Did Wade Gear and Martha Martin attend the same nine-hour meeting in Austin? While Wade Gear was complaining that he felt like he was being pressured to speak on behalf of the Brazos River Authority, Martha Martin was whining that she thought that they had done so. If she was correct, then they violated the law.

To wrap up the summary of the meeting, the presiding officer of the BRA, Mr. Steve Pena, offered his version of the events.

> My comments won't be long. I stayed in that meeting half the day and left a little after noon, I believe. I thought that the morning, uh, the meeting room was congested with about over thirty people. Uh, in the afternoon some of the folks from the senator's office, and from the representative's office, and from the governor's

---

63 Martha Stovall Martin, "Special Board Meeting—Agenda Items 5–6," Brazos River Authority Board of Directors Audio Meetings Minutes, 16:20, March 26, 2007, accessed November 18, 2010. http://brazos.org/board_audio/03262007_1SPL2.mp3.

office, asked if we could just thin out a little bit of the people, which happened.

Um, so, we had fewer people there for the afternoon, and that discussion I was not involved with. But I kept contact with several of the members by phone, uh, or several of the staff, including the governor's office.

I can assure you that the Brazos River Authority went down there with all the intentions of sitting down and talking with the folks about the bill that was being offered. It was our intention all along to work with them. My understanding from this whole process and the folks that I have visited with is that if the land were subject to divestiture, it would be subject to divestiture only at fair market value. And that fair market value would be dependent upon what was actually being transferred. And that is to me dirt and not a piece of paper.

I think that we will see some figures coming up, and these are rough estimates, uh, but I think that what we need to do. And, I think all parties that are interested, and that's not only the governor's office; this is Mr. Keffer's office and certainly Senator Estes' office, who all work with us hand in hand. I think everybody wants to know what exactly we're talking about. And I'm sure the leaseholders want to know exactly what we're talking about.

What would be the difference in passing a bill, or a bill that would pass, that would have, on one hand, the language that includes encumbrances on the land, and on the other hand, unencumbered land? And I think that is a major, significant, and material financial question for the Brazos River Authority. And we've got to know, and I firmly believe this board needs to know, what that difference is. And so with that, I'll save the rest of my comments.[64]

A general discussion followed between Wade Gear and Martha Martin concerning the potential of lawsuits and the fact that the BRA was not a willing seller. Chairman Pena then asked Lauralee Vallon, the chief counsel for the BRA, to provide a statement as to the BRA's position on the legal questions. Lauralee offered the following:

---

64 Steve Pena, "Special Board Meeting—Agenda Items 5–6," Brazos River Authority Board of Directors Audio Meetings Minutes, 17:11, March 26, 2007, accessed November 15, 2010. http://brazos.org/board_audio/03262007_1SPL2.mp3.

Our position has been, at least from the Authority's legal standpoint, that the Constitution provides that we cannot gift assets. We're precluded from giving anything away. So we need to have a fair value for the property. So that sets an established minimum. Our understanding, or at least my understanding from the discussion at that meeting, is what methodology or what language would be put in the bill to articulate or instruct to the appraisers how they would determine the value?

The language that's proposed specifically excludes improvements, and the Brazos River Authority had no objection—at least, you know, theoretically, no objection to that. Because we've acknowledged in our lease form that we allow people, or were planning on in the future potentially allowing people, to recognize they paid for those improvements.

However, with regard to the land, our position is that if the lease extinguishes on the date that the sale actually takes place, if you buy into the Staubach study and the TVA study, which have all found that our leases are undervalued, if you go with what the appraisers, and I think we've got appraisers who are going to go through the process and explain that. But from what we've been advised from the appraisers, they have methodologies that they employ. The standard methodology for an appraiser when he goes out to appraise a piece of property that has a leasehold existing on it, on that day, is to include that value. If the leases are in truth undervalued, that would decrease the underlying value of what's being transferred.

Okay? So our position was that, if you really look at it, it ought to be the unencumbered value of the fee simple, which is the value of the dirt, less the improvements. But that's where we're coming from. I do not know of a law that specifically says it must be this appraisal. As we understand it from talking to the appraisers, those are methodologies that they use in the profession. What we're attempting to do is ensure that if this divestiture legislation does pass, the language is clear enough so that these folks have an instruction of what to do so there's not a lot of time spent at the courthouse, arguing over which methodology would be appropriate.[65]

---

65   Lauralee Vallon, "Special Board Meeting—Agenda Items 5–6," Brazos River Authority Board of Directors Audio Meetings Minutes, 23:56, March 26, 2007, accessed November 23, 2010. http://brazos.org/board_audio/03262007_1SPL2.mp3.

After a bit more banter, Steve Pena offered a final anecdote from the nine-hour meeting.

> Representative Keffer's office brought an appraiser to that meeting. We had never met him. We didn't know he was going to be there. He came there.
>
> Looking at both, and he was asked point-blank by the governor's office and other folks around the table, "Look at the language that the BRA offered, look at the language that has been offered by Mr. Aldrich." And the appraiser said, "Clearly, the language offered by the BRA was much clearer. And the other one was ambiguous."
>
> So, for what that is.[66]

At this point, General Manager Phil Ford turned the podium over to Matt Phillips. Matt was the BRA's Manager of Government and Customer Affairs. He was also a true professional. Any corporate executive who even casually examines his body of work will be impressed with Matt's public relations skills. Throughout the entire process, he never lost his cool, and he genuinely tried to do the next right thing.

Matt endeavored to walk the board members of the Brazos River Authority through the current version of Senate Bill 1326. His remarks were telling.

> Okay, I'm going to explain to you what the document you have in front of you is. This is a draft that came out of Tuesday's meeting. It has not been vetted and/or approved by—and Phil referred to this—by the elected officials' offices involved. They have not signed off on it.
>
> This is just a draft that came out of Tuesday's meeting from the representatives of the PKLPA. They have been doing the majority of a lot of the drafting, and they are the ones that came up with this particular piece of paper.[67]

---

66   Steve Pena, "Special Board Meeting—Agenda Items 5–6," Brazos River Authority Board of Directors Audio Meetings Minutes, 17:11, March 26, 2007, accessed November 15, 2010. http://brazos.org/board_audio/03262007_1SPL2.mp3.

67   Matt Phillips, "Special Board Meeting—Agenda Items 5–6," Brazos River Authority Board of Directors Audio Meetings Minutes, 23:56, March 26, 2007, accessed November 23, 2010. http://brazos.org/board_audio/03262007_1SPL2.mp3.

Board Director Billy Wayne Moore interrupted Matt Phillips to say, "Matt, I just want to make sure I understand clear. This draft came from Representative Keffer's office?"

To which Matt Phillips replied, "No, no, no, no, no. This draft came out of the meeting Tuesday from the representatives from the PKLPA. That's who it came from."

So let me see if I have all of this straight. The governor's office is actively participating in a private negotiation to sell a state asset, and the Possum Kingdom Lake Preservation Association (PKLPA) is drafting the legislation to sell the property to themselves at a discount? BRA board member Wade Gear was adamantly opposed to selling the property at a discount and board member Martha Stovall Martin was convinced that it could all be worked out. The chairman of the BRA wanted nothing short of the fair market value of the land, and the chief counsel of the BRA stated that the Texas Constitution required exactly that.

An hour of discussion followed, with virtually all members stating that they were opposed to divestiture of the property in general and that they were adamantly opposed to selling the property at anything less than the fair market value. A vote was taken at the end of the meeting to document the board's position. The vote was twelve for, one against, and one abstention. The abstention was cast by Martha Stovall Martin.

At the close of business that day, Phil Ford sent another status report to the governor's office.

From: Phil Ford

Sent: Monday, March 26, 2007 4:59 PM

To: Kenneth Anderson; Phil Wilson; Steve Pena

Cc: Matt Phillips; Lauralee Vallon

Subject: FW: revised

Attachments: Substitute Revisions.doc

Gents,

Attached please find a revised version of the proposed committee substitute as drafted by Jay Propes, et al. On Friday, you all received a previous version of these edits based on the concepts discussed during the meeting last Tuesday. The attached version contains most of the same language changes, however, as a result of our

Board meeting today, the valuation section (subsection (d)), has been changed to reflect Board action. The Directors voted to only support divestiture legislation if the language specified that the land will be valued at the fair market value of the unencumbered fee simple estate. The logic behind this decision is explained in the revised substitute. As with the previous document you received, the edits are embedded in the substitute with explanations for each change in green. Matt will send copies of this revised version to both Lewis and Trent. If you have any questions, please give me a call.

Regards,

Phil[68]

Yep, I thought I had that right.

If anyone wants to argue that Governor Perry's office was only casually monitoring the divestiture process, as opposed to actively orchestrating the outcome, I beg to differ. On March 20, 2007, the Eightieth Legislative Session was in full swing, and three of Governor Perry's top lieutenants spent nine hours trying to negotiate a land grab. Ninety-nine percent of the rest of us could not get nine minutes on any of these three men's schedules, much less nine hours during a legislative session. Just ask that lady wearing pink tennis shoes.

At the time of the Austin meeting, Phil Wilson was Governor Perry's deputy chief of staff. On July 1, 2007, Governor Perry appointed Phil Wilson to the position of secretary of state. Rick Perry personally swore Mr. Wilson into office.

Phil Wilson also led the governor's Office of Economic Development and Tourism. "Phil's new role will allow my office to coordinate with the Office of Secretary of State in a seamless way to expand trade, economic development, emerging technology initiatives in the private sector and higher education, and workforce development," Perry said in a 2007 press release.[69]

---

68   Phil Ford, "Substitute Revisions," e-mail message to Kenneth Anderson, Phil Wilson, March 26, 2007, accessed June 11, 2013.

69   "Gov. Perry Names Phil Wilson Texas Secretary of State," Office of the Governor Rick Perry, June 14, 2007, accessed February 1, 2014. http://governor.state.tx.us/news/press-release/2213/.

While serving as secretary of state, Wilson continued to serve as Perry's designee on the Texas Enterprise Fund and the Emerging Technology Fund—two of Rick Perry's favorite and most controversial slush funds for funneling taxpayer dollars to businesses that he favors. In 2010, Governor Rick Perry named Phil Wilson to the oversight committee for the Cancer Prevention and Research Institute of Texas, which is a story that is too long to go into at the moment.

Simultaneously, Ken Anderson was serving as Governor Perry's director of governmental appointments.[70] If you are wondering why the director of appointments would be working a real estate deal for the governor, the answer is simple. Seven of the twenty-one board members' terms were up for reappointment, and Ken Anderson was conducting on-the-job interviews.

The seven members who were appointed in 2001 and whose terms would expire in 2007 were:

1. Martha Stovall Martin,[71]
2. Ronald D. Butler,[72]
3. Fred Lee Hughes,[73]
4. John Skaggs,[74]
5. Suzanne Alderson Baker,[75]

---

70 "Commissioner Kenneth W. Anderson Jr.—Biography," Public Utility Commission of Texas, n.d., accessed February 1, 2014. http://www.puc.texas.gov/agency/about/commissioners/anderson/Biography.aspx.

71 "Martha Stovall Martin—Graham," Board of Directors, Brazos River Authority, n.d., accessed November 14, 2013. http://www.brazos.org/board_bios/martha_martin_bio.pdf.

72 "Ron Butler—Abilene," Board of Directors, Brazos River Authority, n.d., accessed November 14, 2013. http://www.brazos.org/board_bios/ron_butler_bio.pdf.

73 "Fred Lee Hughes—Abilene," Board of Directors, Brazos River Authority, n.d., accessed November 14, 2013. http://www.brazos.org/board_bios/fred_hughes_bio.pdf.

74 "John R. Skaggs—Amarillo," Board of Directors, Brazos River Authority, n.d., accessed November 14, 2013. http://www.brazos.org/board_bios/john_skaggs_bio.pdf.

75 "Suzanne Alderson Baker—Lubbock," Board of Directors, Brazos River Authority, n.d., accessed November 14, 2013. http://www.brazos.org/board_bios/suzanne_baker_bio.pdf.

6. Pamela Jo Ellison,[76] and

7. Salvatore A. Zaccagnino.[77]

While it is certainly possible that the director of governmental appointments was a bit rusty on the laws surrounding the Open Meetings Act, it isn't very likely. In 1993 and 1994, Ken Anderson served as a member of the Rules Advisory Committee of the Texas Ethics Commission during the overhaul of its rules and regulations. This overhaul included the Open Meetings Act. So in other words, a man who helped craft the rules for open meetings was now representing the governor's office to negotiate away a state asset in closed meetings.

That "FYI" e-mail from Phil Ford to Ken Anderson was a warning bark to the Republican hierarchy.

---

76 "P. J. Ellison—Brenham," Board of Directors, Brazos River Authority, n.d., accessed November 14, 2013. http://www.brazos.org/board_bios/pj_ellison_bio.pdf.

77 "Salvatore A. Zaccagnino—Caldwell," Board of Directors, Brazos River Authority, n.d., accessed November 14, 2013. http://www.brazos.org/board_bios/sal_z_bio.pdf.

Chapter 8

THE OPENING HAND

On April 17, 2007, Senator Craig Estes addressed the Senate Natural Resources Committee to explain Senate Bill 1326, which carried the following caption:

"Relating to the sale by the Brazos River Authority of certain residential and commercial lots in the immediate vicinity of Possum Kingdom Lake to leaseholders of those lots."

To set the stage, picture the late Chris Farley, from *Saturday Night Live*, dressed up like Oliver Hardy from the famous comedy duo of Laurel and Hardy. Now take the hat off. If you have that in your mind's eye, then you know what Senator Craig Estes looks like. To complete the image, picture Dana Carvey dressed up like Stan Laurel from the same duo. You now know what Senator Estes's sidekick Jim Keffer looks like. In *The Tale of the River Card*, Senator Estes and Representative Keffer represent the modern-day political version of Laurel and Hardy.

Here is how Senator Estes opened the story of divestiture.[78]

> **Senator Estes:** Thank you, chairman.
>
> Uh, members, this bill is in response to a local issue. Now let me explain that. This is a local issue in the fact that all of these people that we're working with are in my district. What makes it not a local issue is, if this bill is successful, it will be a tremendous windfall of money to the Brazos River Authority, and I know that there are several senators that have Brazos River Authority, uh, in their area.
>
> But this is about Possum Kingdom Lake up in Palo Pinto County, and for those of you unfamiliar with my district, Possum Kingdom Lake is about an hour west of Fort Worth, and it's a scenic and beautiful part of our state, very similar to the hill country around here in Austin. During today's hearing, you'll hear my constituents refer to Possum Kingdom Lake simply as PK or PK Lake.
>
> **Senator Brimer:** Senator, don't sell it too hard. We don't want all these people coming out there.

Because Senator Kim Brimer saw fit to interrupt Senator Estes, let me do the same by reminding you that Brimer was the guy who lost his seat to Wendy Davis, due largely to the rent-to-own scandal, where elected officials laundered campaign contributions into real estate.[79]

> **Estes:** Uh, but for more than sixty-five years, the Brazos River Authority has leased the shoreline property surrounding PK Lake to lessees for residential purposes.
>
> What began as rustic fishing cabins and camper trailers has evolved into a community of primary and secondary residences, some of them quite, uh, expansive, built on sites leased from the BRA.

---

78 Sen. Craig Estes, "Senate Natural Resources Committee," Senate RealMedia Video Archives, Texas Senate, April 17, 2007, accessed May 3, 2013. rtsp://realvideoe.senate. state.tx.us:554/archives/2007/APR/041707.c580.rm.

79 Brad Watson, "Tarrant County Senate Opponents Face Off in Ethics Battle," WFAA-TV, August 15, 2009, accessed December 28, 2013. http://www.wfaa.com/news/local/64502382.html.

Over years and for a variety of reasons, the landlord-lessee relationship has steadily deteriorated between BRA and the residents of PK Lake. My bill provides an opportunity for the leaseholders to pay fair market value to purchase the land under their residences, thus bringing to a mutually beneficial end this ongoing feud between the BRA and the folks that live at PK.

The homeowners will have the security of owning their land, and the BRA will receive financial security from the sale of these lots, while maintaining control of the lake. My office, uh, the BRA, and the representatives of the PK Lake Association and the PK Lake Preservation Association have worked many hours in an effort to reach a consensus, crafting a legislative solution to this local issue.

I want to say a special thanks to Representative Keffer and his staff, who has the companion bill; Governor Perry's office has been involved; Lt. Governor Dewhurst's office for the long time and effort that they've invested in bringing forth this legislation. The result of those cooperative efforts are before you today in the form of this committee substitute.

Stop. If this is a local issue, why are the offices of the governor and lieutenant governor involved? The answer is simple. The lakefront property surrounding Possum Kingdom Lake was by far the most valuable asset that the Brazos River Authority owned. Moreover, there are over eleven million people who live in the Brazos River Basin and over one million people who get their drinking water from the BRA. So we can expect that Governor Rick Perry and Lt. Governor David Dewhurst will be vigorously protecting the interests of the vast number of constituents involved, right?

Over the course of the next thirty-six months, Senator Estes would use the term "local issue" ad nauseam. He would use the term "fair market value" even more often. The point of this case study is to enable readers to make up their own minds as to the validity of those characterizations. Let's continue.

Members, after a recent nine-hour meeting in this building, all parties agreed to the language reflected in this bill. And then, sadly to say, after about a twenty-four-hour period, some people had had second thoughts.

And when I, you know, when agreement is made, uh, to me, it is an agreement. And, uh, that was very disappointing for me. And I was more than a little perturbed at that. But again, I want to say I appreciate everyone who had a hand in helping us craft this compromise. It will be a win-win situation.

And, uh, members, I do want to tell you that to the best of my knowledge, this is the only place in the state of Texas where we have this, uh, situation, and I think it's gonna be a good thing, uh, when … when all parties are cooperatin' and do this.

So, uh, members, I'd be happy to answer your questions, and a lot of them are going to be addressed by those that are here to testify. I do want to say that the main area of contention is the appraisal process. And we have, both sides did not get what they wanted in that, and I, but I think that the appraisal process that we have, as we have it in this bill, is fair to all concerned.

And I'll be happy to go into that in more detail if you'd like for me to.

Thank you, Mr. Chairman.

Stop again. If it is true that a nine-hour meeting was held to negotiate the sale of a multimillion-dollar state asset without a quorum of directors present, and an agreement was indeed reached, then the meeting in reference violated the Texas Open Meetings statutes. So Senator Craig Estes was either misrepresenting the nature of that meeting, or he was confessing to a crime. And who still uses the word perturbed? And by the way, if you are a goat, and you hear a Texas politician using the terms "win-win" and "legislative compromise" in the same paragraph, I suggest you take a look behind you.

After Senator Estes' remarks on the nature of his bill, testimony ensued, beginning with Jay Turner, Robert Upham, and Monte Land. Take note that Lance Byrd, who was "the driving force behind divestiture," was not leading the charge.

Jay Turner was the first to speak. Mr. Turner identified himself as a title attorney from the Dallas area and advised that he had been a leaseholder since 1989. Turner explained to the committee that the adoption of market-oriented rental rates subject to the Staubach Report had caused the lessees to "become organized more fully than they had ever been and pursue divestiture."

He went on to add:

> I was part of that nine-hour meeting that we had here in Austin a awhile, a few weeks ago. And I too, Senator, felt like at the end of the day as we went around the room and the governor's representative asked everyone if we were on board, uh, that we all went around the room and we pretty much were, except representatives of the BRA understandably said they couldn't speak on behalf of the Brazos River Authority Board because they weren't there, represented in total, and would have to get back to us.
>
> And then the next day that … that began to fall apart. So as you said, Senator Estes, the main area of contention is the valuation method.[80]

With those comments, Jay Turner introduced some clarity into the confusion. According to Turner, the nine-hour meeting held in Austin was only an attempt to circumvent the open-meeting statutes, as opposed to a successful effort to do so. Of course, merely attempting to violate those statutes is also illegal. Turner also reinforced the fact that the primary problem to be solved was how to value the land that the BRA was being forced to sell.

At this point, Senator Estes interrupted the witness to inform his fellow committee members of another bill that he had in the works. He stated for the record:

> And members let me interject here, since he brings that up, if I may.
>
> I have a bill to reduce the members on the BRA board that we're going to be looking at, maybe in a few days. But, there are twenty-one members now on the board, and there was a vote … uh, let's see. Special board meeting voted to recommend a different language than was agreed at the nine-hour meeting and, uh, the

---

80   Jay Turner, "Senate Natural Resources Committee," Senate RealMedia Video Archives, 4:16:11, Texas Senate, April 17, 2007, accessed July 9, 2013. rtsp://realvideoe.senate.state. tx.us:554/archives/2007/APR/041707.c580.rm.

vote was twelve yes to one no, one abstention, and there were seven absent.

So to me that suggests that there might be some disagreement or maybe some ambivalence among some of the directors as to their position on the bill.

Necessity will require that we explore the sentiments of the Brazos River Authority Board during the special meeting that Estes referred to. What is important to recognize about this interruption is that Estes never missed an opportunity to state publicly that he was more than prepared to overhaul the Brazos River Authority Board—or eliminate it entirely, if that was what it took to get what he wanted.

After a digression by Jay Turner as to the difference between a fee simple estate and a leasehold estate, committee chairman Kip Averitt posed the obvious question.

Well, I have a question, if I might.

I, uh, I don't understand. According to you, the folks who are leasing the property suggest one way to determine what a fair price would be, and the Brazos River Authority has another way of determining what a fair price would be. *Surely* there's somebody out there that's independent and objective and, uh, someone that, or a group of someone's that can be agreed upon in advance that would render an opinion as to the proper way to value the property.[81]

Jay Turner's response was succinct: "I would hope that would be the appraisal community."

Before Turner could continue, Senator Estes attempted to establish that if no one got what he or she wanted, then Estes' compromise must be fair.

Uh, Mr. Chairman, if I may jump in here …

It's kind of splitting hairs on … on phraseology. What the Lake Association wanted was the phrase "fair market value for interest

81 Sen. Kip Averitt, "Senate Natural Resources Committee," Senate RealMedia Video Archives, 4:20:51, Texas Senate, April 17, 2007, accessed July 9, 2013. rtsp://realvideoe. senate.state.tx.us:554/archives/2007/APR/041707.c580.rm.

being acquired." Uh, what the BRA wanted was "fair market value
for the unencumbered fee simple estate." The compromise was,
and we've talked to a lot of appraisers on this, and the compromise
was, it's on page 3 line 4, "a lot sold under this section must be sold
for not less than the fair market value of the land."

To the average Joe, the difference between the phrase "fair market
value for the unencumbered fee simple estate" and the phrase "fair market
value of the land" might seem negligible. Of course, if that were true, we
wouldn't have this big damn disagreement or a room full of some of the
most expensive lawyers in Texas.

To an appraiser, an "unencumbered fee simple estate" is easy to
appraise. In the case of Possum Kingdom Lake, you would simply look
at that sweet piece of lakefront property and pretend that there was not
a $1 million home sitting on it. You would then ask yourself this simple
question: What is an acre of raw lakefront property going for these days
in the state of Texas? And then you are done.

For some reason, the good Lord saw fit to limit the number of
naturally occurring lakes in the entire, vast state of Texas to exactly
one. That would be Caddo Lake. Every other lake in the state is man-
made. Stated differently, I think that it is fair to say that the inventory
of lakefront property in Texas is somewhat limited. Consequently, most
would conclude that lakefront property in the state of Texas is unusually
valuable, relatively speaking.

On the other hand, the phrase "fair market value of the land" has
virtually no legal meaning in the appraisal community that Jay Turner
referred to, and this is exactly what Senator Estes and the weekenders
wanted—total ambiguity. There is no telling what an appraiser who makes
his living appraising land in Palo Pinto County for his neighbors might
consider to be the "fair market value of the land" without some guidelines.
I would respectfully submit that the difference between these two phrases
approximates a canyon large enough to turn into a rather nice lake. It ain't
splitting hairs.

Estes was not done with his efforts to muddy the water. He went on to
explain his proposed three-step appraisal process. Step 1: The leaseholder
gets an appraisal. Step 2: If the BRA considers the appraisal to be a

brother-in-law–looking deal, then the BRA can pay for a second appraisal. Step 3: If the leaseholder considers the BRA's appraisal to look like full retail, the leaseholder can request that the comptroller's office pay for a third appraisal that would be required to come in at plus or minus 5 percent of the median of the first two appraisals.

What kind of bullshit deal is that? Under this scenario, the state of Texas could fully expect to have to pay for two separate professional appraisals on each and every transaction, while the leaseholder could fully expect to have to give his brother-in-law a six pack of beer. And when all is said and done, you can bet your ass that the Texas taxpayers are going to wind up with a sales price that magically approximates seventy-five cents on the dollar, if they are lucky.

To put a final coat of lipstick on his pig, Senator Estes offered one more comment during Jay Turner's testimony: "I don't want anything but a fair, fair price for the people of Texas who really own this land. In my opinion, the BRA is the custodian for those people."

Uh, would that not make this a Texas issue, rather than a local issue?

The next gentleman to testify was Mr. Robert Upham, who was representing the Possum Kingdom Lake Preservation Association (PKLPA). While the Possum Kingdom Lake Association (PKLA) had positioned itself as the official mouthpiece of the leaseholders, they were the minor leaguers compared to the PKLPA.

Senator Estes introduced Robert Upham in the following fashion:

> "By the way, as we go to our next witness, uh, Mr. Upham has
> been, uh, chairman of the board of the Brazos River Authority in
> years past, not too long ago. Go ahead, sir."

As a reminder, Robert Upham is the son of Chester R. Upham, the man who is credited with starting the Republican Party of Texas in a phone booth. He was the son of a kingmaker. Not surprisingly, the Upham estate at Possum Kingdom Lake rests on Upham Drive. As we say in Texas, go big or go home. In this deal, Robert Upham was as big as they come, especially with Rick Perry entertaining ideas about a run for the White House.

> Yes, sir. My name is Robert Upham. I served on the BRA board
> from 1981 to 1993, sir. I was appointed by Governor Clements,
> and I reside in Mineral Wells in Palo Pinto County. And I had
> the pleasure of serving on the board with Senator Brimer for a few
> years before he ran his campaign for the House.
>
> I am the chairman of the Possum Kingdom Lake Preservation
> Association, and we are here in support of Senator Estes' bill,
> 1326, and we appreciate your consideration of the bill. We are in
> favor of it, and … we've put a lot of effort into, hoping to … to
> gain passage of this legislation to afford the lessees to purchase
> their land, their lots. I think it will be a win-win for both the
> lessees and the BRA.[82]

Robert Upham's testimony lasted a mere three minutes. Here was a
guy who actually served as the chairman of the Brazos River Authority
for twelve years, and nobody bothered to ask, "How in the hell did we get
into this mess?" Likewise, nobody asked him to split any hairs on what he
thought would be a fair way to value the property. You simply do not put
a man like this on the spot in public testimony.

The next to speak was Monte Land, the chairman of the Possum
Kingdom Lake Association. At the risk of being condescending, Monte
Land was the coach of the minor league organization. Here are few
highlights from his remarks.

> My wife and I are retired public school teachers who have owned
> property at Possum Kingdom for the last, oh, probably the past
> thirty-two years. We bought property at Possum Kingdom with
> the idea of retiring out there. This was in 1975 when we first
> invested out there.
>
> I'm also president of the Possum Kingdom Lake Association,
> which is an association of all of the different people that live out
> at the lake. … We have approximately nine hundred dues-paying
> members to the association.
>
> I'm here to ask for your support of the bill, like Mr. Upham
> here …

---

82 Robert Upham, "Senate Natural Resources Committee," Senate RealMedia Video
    Archives, 4:34:33, Texas Senate, April 17, 2007, accessed July 9, 2013. rtsp://realvideoe.
    senate.state.tx.us:554/archives/2007/APR/041707.c580.rm.

> I think all of this came about … when the board of the Brazos River decided to change their methodology for lease rates.
>
> If that leasing program continues, my wife and I will not be able to stay at the lake. We will be priced out. … The lease will break me.[83]

Monte Land continued to poor-mouth the committee members for a while longer about the impending impact of the proposed graduated rental increases on the dream retirement that he and his wife had crafted. Finally, Chairman Kip Averitt asked the obvious question in regard to Monte Land's annual rent: "What is it currently?"

To which Monte Land replied: "Uh, I don't even know."

Consider me officially pissed off. You show up in front of a Texas Senate Committee, looking for a handout, and have the nerve/balls to testify that you don't even know what you are currently paying in rent. Let me help you out on this one, Mr. Land. You were paying $800 per year. The appraisal district's assessed value on the lakefront property that was owned by the state of Texas that you and Mrs. Land were occupying was assessed at $74,050 in 2008. The cottage that you and your wife built was assessed at $400,000 in the same year. Damn, I wish I was a poor, retired school teacher who needed protection from the Texas legislature.

And then, as fast as Monte Land says that he doesn't know what he is paying in rent, he offers up that he is paying $800 per year. I guess he was too embarrassed to admit that he was only paying $67 per month for almost a full acre of lakefront property. Given that I pay over $130 per month for a tiny U-Haul space that serves no other purpose than to store the annual Christmas decorations, my daughter's collection of American Girl dolls and Snow Babies, and a bunch of other crap that my wife refuses to part with, I get it.

After these three gentlemen testified, the podium was turned over to the individuals who were sworn to uphold the interest of the taxpayers of the state of Texas.

---

83 Monte Land, "Senate Natural Resources Committee," Senate RealMedia Video Archives, 4:37:38, Texas Senate, April 17, 2007, accessed July 9, 2013. rtsp://realvideoe. senate.state.tx.us:554/archives/2007/APR/041707.c580.rm.

Chairman Averitt called Ms. Lauralee Vallon, Mr. Matt Phillips, Mr. Phil Ford, and Mr. Steve Pena to the witness table. Ms. Lauralee Vallon served as the general counsel of the Brazos River Authority. She was a paid staffer. Mr. Matt Phillips served as the manager of Government and Customer Relations of the Brazos River Authority. He was a paid staffer. Mr. Phil Ford served as the general manager/CEO of the Brazos River Authority. He was a paid staffer. Mr. Steve Pena served as the presiding officer of the Brazos River Authority board of directors and was appointed by Governor Rick Perry.

Steve Pena was the first to speak.

> Mr. Chairman, members of the committee, good afternoon. My name is Steve Pena. I'm chairman of the board of directors of the Brazos River Authority. And with me today is Mr. Phil Ford, Lauralee Vallon, and Matt Phillips. I'm here today to testify on behalf of our board, concerning the committee substitute to Senate Bill 1326.
>
> Suffice it to say our board has spent considerable time discussing the divestiture of property and best practices for land management at Possum Kingdom, and we basically concluded that it was not in the best interest of the Brazos River Authority or its customers to divest of property at PK.
>
> Having said that, we received feedback from members of the legislature, from lessees at Possum Kingdom, and from the governor's office. And based on that feedback, we decided to revisit our decision on the issue.
>
> I know our board earnestly wants to cooperate with the desires of the legislature. However, in doing so, we firmly believe that we must protect the Brazos River Authority and its customers from the sale of an asset below value. We have been diligently working with Senator Estes to determine whether there is a way to address divestiture that would reduce any adverse impact to the Brazos River Authority system and to its customers. And we appreciate his willingness to work with us on these issues.
>
> The fact that the sale of this asset affects the entire Brazos River Authority Basin makes the assertion, however, that this is a local issue misleading. This is not a local bill, as it will have an effect on the price that the Brazos River Authority charges to provide water.

While we plan to continue working on a solution, we are opposed
to the committee substitute in its current form.[84]

Steve Pena went on to enumerate several reasons why the Brazos River
Authority was opposed to Senate Bill 1326. The BRA's position is most
clearly depicted in his final point.

> Finally and to reiterate, after working with all parties, we believe
> the most significant issue remaining is that of ensuring the land
> be sold at a fair and equitable price.
>
> The language in the committee's substitute provides that the
> property will be sold for the "fair market value of the land." But
> after consulting with two independent appraisal firms and those
> firms assuming a willing buyer and a willing seller transaction.
>
> And I'll stop at my prepared remarks, senators, to say that this is
> not a willing buyer/willing seller transaction. In a market value
> scenario, the selling and the buying parties have full knowledge
> of all the facts and are not under any pressure to either buy or
> sell. But that is not the case here. The BRA is being told to sell
> and being told to sell, in our opinion, way below market value of
> the land.
>
> We request that language be included requiring the land to be
> appraised for the fair market value of the unencumbered fee simple
> estate. The BRA is being asked to convey fee simple title. Why
> should we not ask for a fee simple price?

I am finding it hard to characterize the BRA as ambivalent. An
exchange ensued between Senator Kim Brimer and Steve Pena concerning
the impact of appraisers discounting the property for the value of the
existing leases and the fact that the leases would terminate upon the sale
of each individual lot. Senator Estes interrupted yet again by saying:

> But, Steve-O, that's not what it says. It says "the value of the land."
> And might some appraiser, one appraiser look at it differently from
> another appraiser?

84 Steve Pena, "Senate Natural Resources Committee," Senate RealMedia Video Archives,
4:49:36, Texas Senate, April 17, 2007, accessed July 9, 2013. rtsp://realvideoe.senate.
state.tx.us:554/archives/2007/APR/041707.c580.rm.

I'm talking about the language that it is right now. We didn't put the language in that the leaseholders wanted. We didn't put the language in you wanted. We came with a compromise language that y'all signed off on and then you went back and decided you didn't like it.

But I guess the question is, might different appraisers see that language that's in there right now, uh, some are going to see it your way, some are going to see it their way. Am I wrong about that? Tell me where I'm wrong.[85]

No, Senator Estes, you are not wrong. You are simply an idiot for expecting the rest of us to buy off on your attempt to legislate ambiguity. Of course, different appraisers will interpret the language differently. That is the f*&^%#@ problem!

At this point, Lauralee Vallon, the BRA's chief counsel explained that the BRA had specifically asked their two independent appraisers to evaluate Estes' compromise language. Both firms stated that, unless instructed otherwise, any appraiser would be required to discount the property by the value of the existing lease and ignore the fact that the lease would terminate upon the property's transfer. To this statement, Senator Estes simply replied, "Okay, thank you."

Chairman Averitt then rejoined the discussion by saying, "Senator Estes, I know how hard you've worked on this."[86] To which Estes replied, "We can go another nine hours if you want to, Chairman."

Averitt continued:

I know how hard you've been working on this. But you know, what I was trying to get to earlier, and I think it's getting flushed out here, is that apparently the language in the bill can be interpreted by an appraiser any number of different ways, and I think that, I think that there should be some certainty as to the methodology that the appraiser approaches this process, and I don't think that's contrary to what your objective is.

---

85   Sen. Craig Estes, "Senate Natural Resources Committee," Senate RealMedia Video Archives, 5:00:23, Texas Senate, April 17, 2007, accessed July 9, 2013. rtsp://realvideoe. senate.state.tx.us:554/archives/2007/APR/041707.c580.rm.

86   Sen. Kip Averitt, "Senate Natural Resources Committee," Senate RealMedia Video Archives, 5:00:23, Texas Senate, April 17, 2007, accessed July 10, 2013. rtsp://realvideoe. senate.state.tx.us:554/archives/2007/APR/041707.c580.rm.

Senator Ken Brimer attempted to come to Senator Estes' aid by adding his own spin to the record.

> Senator Averitt, I've been studying this, and knowing what the value of real estate is along the Brazos River for unimproved raw land, it seems like that's where we need to go. Whatever the value is of land along the Brazos that's unimproved would fit this criteria. And when you take all the amenities out, I know that that stuff has doubled in the last five to six years, fortunately for my family, but uh, I mean you're looking at values anywhere from asking price of $3,000 to $6,000 nowadays for an acre. And that seems like what we're looking at—an acre value of raw land.[87]

Given that Senator Kim Brimer had served on the Brazos River Authority board at the same time as Robert Upham, you would think that he might have had a bit more situational awareness with regard to Possum Kingdom Lake. Comparing waterfront property along the Brazos River to waterfront property on Possum Kingdom Lake is laughable. And BRA board chairman Steve Pena politely said so in reply. If you were to take a canoe trip from the dam at Possum Kingdom Lake south to Lake Granbury, there are places that you would have to carry the damn thing during a drought. On the other hand, Possum Kingdom is one of the deepest lakes in Texas. On Possum Kingdom Lake, your canoe might get swamped by a sixty-foot yacht.

At about this point, Senator Estes stated his conclusions to BRA chairman Steve Pena.

> We've heard ranges for what you're going to get from this the sale between $35 million to $200 million. Let's say it is $60 million. That would be on the low side. At 5 percent, that would be $3 million per year, so that would be double what you're making now.
>
> I'm pretty convinced we've got a fair deal, but you know people can disagree on things. But I appreciated working with you. You guys have been fun to work with. We just haven't agreed on anything.

---

87   Sen. Kim Brimer, "Senate Natural Resources Committee," Senate RealMedia Video Archives, 5:02:55, Texas Senate, April 17, 2007, accessed July 10, 2013. rtsp://realvideoe. senate.state.tx.us:554/archives/2007/APR/041707.c580.rm.

Chairman Pena tried one more time to help Senator Estes understand the problems related to the ambiguity of his proposed language in the bill.

> Sixty million dollars seems like a large number and in fact, it is. So is $200 million. And so the difference between there is obviously $140 million, and that's rolling the dice with the people's asset and future value.[88]

The next two gentlemen called to the podium were Robert Aldrich and Joe Staley. Both were representing the Possum Kingdom Lake Preservation Association.

For the most part, Mr. Aldrich's remarks reiterated what Jay Turner, Robert Upham, and Monte Land already had stated. He did add, however, that an economic study had been performed in 2005 by a Palo Pinto accountant by the name of Dennis Cannedy, which clearly demonstrated that selling the lakefront property would be economically beneficial to the BRA. Senator Estes commented that he was familiar with Mr. Cannedy, which drew some awkward laughter. Senator Estes failed to mention, for the record, that Dennis Cannedy was his campaign treasurer.

Joe Staley's testimony was related to the Set Ranch that was part of the property in contention. The Set Ranch had its own unique set of valuation problems, and Mr. Staley stated multiple times in multiple ways that the law was on the side of the leaseholders.

This concluded the first round of public testimony on Senate Bill 1326. At this point, Chairman Averitt read the witness cards for those who were for or against the bill but did not wish to testify. Among those in favor of the bill, wishing to remain silent, were Rebecca Lucas and future Tarrant County district attorney Joe Shannon. The last person identified as being for the bill but not wishing to testify was Lance Byrd, the River Card's "inspiration for getting involved." Don't you love those people who lead the charge from the rear?

Senate Bill 1326 was left pending in committee.

---

88   Steve Pena, "Senate Natural Resources Committee," Senate RealMedia Video Archives, 5:12:09, Texas Senate, April 17, 2007, accessed July 10, 2013. rtsp://realvideoe.senate. state.tx.us:554/archives/2007/APR/041707.c580.rm.

Chapter 9

THE MISSED DEAL

The best fishing stories are usually about the ones that got away. Here's your fish story.

On April 23, 2007, six days after the original Senate Committee hearing, the Senate Natural Resources Committee reconvened at the desk of Senator Kip Averitt on the floor of the Texas Senate. As a consequence, there is no video archive of this meeting, only audio minutes, which contain some small gaps of inaudible testimony.

The chairman of the committee, Senator Kip Averitt, explained that there were four bills that could not get out of committee on April 17 because there was no quorum present. To expedite matters, he called the members to his desk on the floor of the Senate, established a quorum, and proceeded to move things along.

Four minutes into the impromptu meeting, Chairman Averitt turned to Senate Bill 1326 and read the caption.

> Senate Bill 1326 by Estes relating to the sale by the Brazos River Authority of certain residential and commercial lots in the immediate vicinity of Possum Kingdom Lake to leaseholders of those lots.

We have not adopted the committee substitute. Therefore, Senator Estes moves that we adopt the committee substitute that we had laid out. Is there any objection?

The chair hears none, and the substitute is adopted. Senator Estes is working on the bill still. It is not in its final form by any means. He's coming up with a whole new way to divert, uh, get the BRA to divest of that property, uh, and we will expect to be seeing that in the near future.

But in the meantime in order to keep the process rolling, uh, that's where we are.

And therefore, Senator Estes moves that Senate Bill 1326 not pass but the committee substitute adopted in lieu thereof do pass and be printed. The clerk will call the roll.[89]

The vote was by no means unanimous. As the eleven senators were polled, Senator Duncan replied, "Not yet," while Senator Glenn Hegar replied, "I'm here," and Senator Uresti replied, "Present." The final tally was eight ayes, one nay, and two present not voting. Based on that vote, Chairman Averitt declared Senate Bill 1326 to be favorably reported. Given the absence of a unanimous vote, Senate Bill 1326 would now be sent to the Senate floor to be voted on by the entire thirty-one–member body of the Senate. Make a note that State Senator Glenn Hegar passed on the opportunity to vote one way or the other on Senate Bill 1326.

Four days later, on Sunday, April 27, 2007, BRA general manager Phil Ford called an emergency meeting of the BRA board. The only order of business was titled "Response to Proposed Language for Committee Substitute to Senate Bill 1326 Pursuant to Legislative Inquiries."

The emergency meeting began with an anguished explanation from CEO Phil Ford as to the purpose of the meeting. He relayed that he had received several phone calls over the past few days from Austin, and that Senator Averitt and Senator Estes had a handshake deal to change the language of the bill. "And that's what we're here to discuss."

The next to speak was Matt Phillips, the manager of Customer and Government Affairs for the BRA. Matt provided a lengthy explanation

---

89   Sen. Kip Averitt, "Senate Natural Resources Committee," Senate RealMedia Video Archives, 3:50, Texas Senate, April 23, 2007, accessed July 10, 2013. rtsp://realvideoe. senate.state.tx.us:554/archives/2007/APR/042307.c580.rm.

of the proposed new language of SB 1326 and the implications to the financial welfare of the Brazos River Authority. The crux of the matter was this: the leaseholders wanted a discount on the property that they were trying to buy, because the property was currently encumbered by a lease, even though each lease would terminate upon the sale of the properties.

Nineteen minutes into the meeting, Director Wade Gear and Director Billy Wayne Moore attempted to summarize the comments of Mr. Ford and Mr. Phillips with the following exchange.

> **Director Gear:** Basically, we're being asked—correct me if I'm wrong—how much money is it acceptable for the BRA to leave on the table.
>
> **Director Moore:** We are being asked, how much are we going to give away? I understand the term "leave on the table," but a lot of people don't.
>
> **Gear:** I can carry it one step further. We are being asked to assist in gutting a state agency, and my hands aren't going to be on that knife.
>
> **Moore:** Mine either.
>
> **Gear:** I was in Austin, and I am so sick of the process. Um, fair market value at the unencumbered fee simple estate is what this board accepted. I'm not going to vote for anything else.
>
> Now, what Phil and the staff is bringing forward to us is what Senator Averitt and everybody is trying to appease the BRA with and to get things through. I can't tell you how many times somebody has set up from elsewhere, including my senator, and said this is going to be good for the BRA. But every time I turn around it's, "You know, we're going to hurt ya; it just depends on how much we're gonna hurt ya."
>
> And Lauralee is going to shoot me when I say this, but they are picking and choosing portions of the law and portions of the appraisal process that best suit their purpose. When you appraise a lease-fee property, Texas case law holds—Lauralee, correct me if I'm wrong—that the owner of the property has a general assumption when the lease is silent to it, to expect that those improvements revert to his ownership at the end of the term of the lease. So if you've got somebody with a one-year lease and a million-dollar house on it, that house has value to the BRA if

they want to use that appraisal process. And what they've done by putting "fair market value of the land" is take that out because they've said, "Well, we built that house; you have no right to the house."

I hear what they're saying, and I don't want their house, but let's not pick and choose the portions of the law that best benefit the lessee. And that's exactly what's taking place.

Moore: Can we back the buggy up two steps? Number one, none of this land has been declared surplus. And number two, in my opinion, we are an unwilling seller. And number three, I think this sale sets a very dangerous precedent for legislative efforts to divest state land for special interests and the next state park for sale. I want it![90]

Matt Phillips let out a heavy sigh and asked, "Okay, do you want me to continue with the changes or go on?" With a few nods, he continued to explain the changes to the bill. The next major change was that those leaseholders who did not want to purchase their property would be allowed to continue leasing. As the primary pretense that Senator Estes had repeatedly used for pushing divestiture was to get the BRA out of the land management business, this sent a few of the board members into orbit, especially Wade Gear.

> My understanding of the original purpose of the bill was to get the BRA out of the land management business. Now by taking Subsection G out, it places us right smack back in the land management business, and all it does is create a scenario whereby the rich people can afford their place, they get to buy it, and we get to deal with everybody else.[91]

90   Wade Gear, "Emergency Board Meeting—Agenda Items 5–6," Brazos River Authority Board of Directors Audio Meetings Minutes, 19:00, April 27, 2007, accessed July 10, 2013. http://brazos.org/board_audio/04272007_EME2.mp3.

91   Wade Gear, "Emergency Board Meeting—Agenda Items 5–6," Brazos River Authority Board of Directors Audio Meetings Minutes, 24:58, April 27, 2007, accessed July 10, 2013. http://brazos.org/board_audio/04272007_EME2.mp3.

At this point, Matt Phillips introduced another option that General Manager Phil Ford had referred to earlier as a "handshake" deal between Senator Estes and Senator Averitt.

> There's been, I don't want to say offered, but there's been discussed the possibility of another option—an option that's more simple, that does not have convoluted schemes to it, that does not have equations. The option would be that the land would be appraised for its unencumbered fee simple value with a 10 percent offset for the value of the leasehold interest. ...
>
> That's what we've been asked to ensure is the only, that that's as far as we go. We've been asked that by other members [of the House] to ensure that that is as far as we go as far as giving any sort of discount and/or offset. ...
>
> So what that does, when we ran the averages on all of our leases, and we have an average age eighteen-year term, based on average values, it was our understanding that the language in the bill, as written, could have led us to, if it were to pass as is, could lead us to losing 49 percent of the value. Am I correct on that? In this equation, if this language is offered as a possibility, and like I said, it has been *discussed*, we ensure that on every transaction, on every one of these, its 90 percent of the unencumbered value, no matter what.[92]

To which Wade Gear responded, "So, 10 percent means that we would leave $20 million on the table?" Phillips continued. He knew that this was the best deal that the BRA was ever going to see on the table and he sold it hard.

> You know, and that is correct. That is one way to look at it. But if the bill were to pass as is, we could leave $100 million on the table. And what I would say to you, with all due respect to everybody here, is that the actions of the legislature are independent of the actions of our board. We know what we want to do, but that doesn't mean that they're going to do what we want them to do. We could see a bill that could be horrible for us.

---

92   Matt Phillips, "Emergency Board Meeting—Agenda Items 5–6," Brazos River Authority Board of Directors Audio Meetings Minutes, 28:50, April 27, 2007, accessed July 10, 2013. http://brazos.org/board_audio/04272007_EME2.mp3.

But we are being asked at this time, we have been included in the room throughout this entire process. We could have, at the outset, stomped our feet, took our toys, and gone home and said, "We're not going to play." And we could have ended up with whatever they want to pass. Through this process, by participating within it, we have been able to at least attempt to ensure that this bill does not hurt us as much as it could.

Matt's sales pitch was met with both appreciation and contempt. Nonetheless, Wade Gear defended his position against discounts.

You know, in defense of Phil and his staff, they have done their jobs. They have been involved in the process. They have worked it to the best of their ability. They have been as frustrated, if not more frustrated, than I have. But as a board member, I'm not going to negotiate away a state asset.

I hear what Matt is saying, that we're trying to keep, we're trying to mold our future. But I, you know, leaving money on the table is unacceptable when it benefits a wealthy contingency.

And I apologize. I have got to get to a client meeting. But from my standpoint, I don't want my fingerprints anything on discounts.

After more discussion on math, legal precedents, and multiple comments about being an unwilling seller, a woman who would become the voice of reason for the BRA board finally weighed in on the matters at hand. This voice was that of Carolyn Johnson, who joined the board in 2005.[93] While she may have been new to the arguments, she was absolutely nobody's fool.

Well, I have a comment. When we last left, I was very, I was not very pleased, but I thought that this thing had a very low chance of getting out of committee. And since they did such a roundabout way to get it out of committee, I think now that I, it might have a better chance that it might pass. And knowing that something like this might pass, we have to do what we can to protect BRA.

93　Judi Pierce, "Gov. Perry Appoints Six Individuals to Brazos River Authority Board of Directors," Brazos River Authority, April 25, 2005, accessed February 1, 2014. http://www.brazos.org/newsPdf/5-6-2005_New_Directors.pdf.

And if giving up 10 percent is the way to do it, then I think we have to really strongly consider.

Now, I agree with you, Wade, that we don't want to leave anything on the table, but we also have to know if there's a chance of it passing, then we've got to do something to protect us because we don't want to give away 50 percent of it. So that's, we need to really think closely and carefully about whether or not we want to support something like the 10 percent discount because that's a whole lot better, in the long run. It's just my comment.[94]

While Carolyn Johnson may have been the voice of reason, Director Pamela (P. J.) Ellison was the voice of passion. P. J. spoke next.

Well, and my comment is, and I try not to be too Pollyanna-ish here, and I certainly don't want to do anything to make staff's lives harder than it already is, but I have a major, major problem when the governor's office is directing people not to be at hearings, not to speak.

I have a major problem when this boils down to, we are, not only, it's not whether you're going to get raped or not; it's just at what extreme are you going to?[95]

In hindsight, the answer to that question would be, "Like a tied-up goat."

The impact of that question was as profound as it was jarring. Prior to that question, General Manager Phil Ford had been corresponding with Governor Perry's top lieutenants as to the progress of the drafting of the bill and to the BRA's position on the bill. From that day forward, all written correspondence between the governor's office and the BRA ceased. Henceforth, it was phone calls only.

P. J. Ellison continued:

---

94 Carolyn Johnson, "Emergency Board Meeting—Agenda Items 5–6," Brazos River Authority Board of Directors Audio Meetings Minutes, 36:19, April 27, 2007, accessed July 11, 2013. http://brazos.org/board_audio/04272007_EME2.mp3.

95 P. J. Ellison, "Emergency Board Meeting—Agenda Items 5–6," Brazos River Authority Board of Directors Audio Meetings Minutes, 37:23, April 27, 2007, accessed July 11, 2013. http://brazos.org/board_audio/04272007_EME2.mp3.

And I'm sorry for being passionate about this, but I'm being asked to compromise the people of Texas just to make senators happy. What happened to the people doing the right thing for the people? I have a real problem with being asked to compromise my integrity. I'm sorry.

And Carolyn, I agree with you, and Wade, I agree with you. I don't know. I don't know what we need to do. But I cannot sit at this table and say, "Okay. It's okay to do this."

Billy Wayne Moore chimed in next. "The first thing that we need to do is make them aware that whatever they do, we are an unwilling seller." To that, someone else replied, "We sure don't want to go on record as being party to or a writer of the bill."

Ever the professional diplomat, Matt Phillips offered this:

We have been very clear throughout this process that the transaction created through this bill is not willing buyer, willing seller. Which is why, because of the provisions of the bill, we've worked to try to change them. We've said that, "This is not willing buyer, willing seller. But if you're going to pass it, it has to be a close as possible."[96]

General Manager Phil Ford then attempted to frame the decision in the simplest of terms.

Let me make another point. Trust me, I've been, I've been, I've been Wade. I've been Bob. I've been P. J. I've been Carolyn, trying to fight through this almost hostage negotiation while trying to make sure that people don't killed or left in the wake of somebody that's got a gun.

And so, and then how do you look at yourself when you shave? Ninety percent of something is worth more than forty percent of zero.

---

96   Matt Phillips, "Emergency Board Meeting—Agenda Items 5–6," Brazos River Authority Board of Directors Audio Meetings Minutes, 38:49, April 27, 2007, accessed July 12, 2013. http://brazos.org/board_audio/04272007_EME2.mp3.

Everything we've said here is as truthful as we can make it.[97]

And then Wade Gear finally asked the key question: "Have the Jays chimed in on the 10 percent?"[98]

Gear was referring to Jay Propes and Jay Brown, the lobbyists from the Graydon Group representing the Possum Kingdom Lake Preservation Association. As noted earlier by Phil Ford, Jay Propes was actually drafting Senate Bill 1326. Without their consent, this entire discussion was a total waste of time.

Thereafter, the tone of the meeting alternated from disgust to dismay to disbelief. The consensus among the thirteen directors present that day was clear. They were adamantly opposed to divestiture in general and specifically opposed to selling prime real estate to a wealthy contingency at a discount. At the forty-four–minute mark, the following exchange occurred:

> **Director John Skaggs:** Matt, let me just throw out my two bits worth. I've been sitting here listening to PK arguments for six years now, and I've heard about everything there is to be said, I do believe. And I agree with all of us. I feel the same way Wade does. I feel the same way Carolyn does. The political reality is the legislature passes laws all the time that hurt people. And they're not fair. They do it all the time. And they're getting ready to do it to us.
>
> **Director Jean Kilgore:** Yes, but we're being asked to put our approval on it. We're their alibi.
>
> **Skaggs:** It won't matter whether we approve it or not. They're going to do what they want to do.
>
> **Kilgore:** I know it. But if we vote to approve it, then we are their alibi. Then it comes back on us.[99]

---

97 Phil Ford, "Emergency Board Meeting—Agenda Items 5–6," Brazos River Authority Board of Directors Audio Meetings Minutes, 41:28, April 27, 2007, accessed July 12, 2013. http://brazos.org/board_audio/04272007_EME2.mp3.

98 Wade Gear, "Emergency Board Meeting—Agenda Items 5–6," Brazos River Authority Board of Directors Audio Meetings Minutes, 42:48, April 27, 2007, accessed July 12, 2013. http://brazos.org/board_audio/04272007_EME2.mp3.

99 John Skaggs, "Emergency Board Meeting—Agenda Items 5–6," Brazos River Authority Board of Directors Audio Meetings Minutes, 44:00, April 27, 2007, accessed July 12, 2013. http://brazos.org/board_audio/04272007_EME2.mp3.

The more they talked, the more they realized that accepting a forced sale at a forced discount of a specified amount would be the least of all evils. The discussion turned to how much they should leave on the table. Since 10 percent was the starting point, the debate involved whether they should ask for only a 5 percent discount.

Matt Phillips settled the matter in five words: "Trust me. They want thirty."[100]

Based on the estimates from the Staubach Report, it was widely accepted that the collective value of the lakefront lots was in the neighborhood of $200 million. A 10 percent discount would effectively leave $20 million on the table. A 30 percent discount would leave $60 million on the table. However, the constructs of the bill as it was currently written threatened a forced sale that would potentially leave $100 million on the table. In reality, those estimates were incredibly low.

The debate resulted in a resolution that read as follows:

Brazos River Authority

RESOLUTION OF THE BOARD OF DIRECTORS OF

THE BRAZOS RIVER AUTHORITY

APRIL 27, 2007

Agenda Item 5

Response to the Proposed Language for Committee Substitute

To Senate Bill 1326 pursuant to Legislative Inquiries

The following resolution is presented for consideration to the Board of Directors of the Brazos River Authority for adoption at the April 27, 2007, meeting.

WHEREAS the Brazos River Authority Board of Directors fundamentally is opposed to divestiture of its landholdings at Possum Kingdom Lake, due to the overriding principals of stewardship and preservation; and

WHEREAS the Brazos River Authority has communicated its concerns openly and in good faith to the State Legislature throughout this process; and

---

100 Matt Phillips, "Emergency Board Meeting—Agenda Items 5–6," Brazos River Authority Board of Directors Audio Meetings Minutes, 1:23:34, April 27, 2007, accessed July 12, 2013. http://brazos.org/board_audio/04272007_EME2.mp3.

WHEREAS, the Board of Directors is committed to ensuring the best policy practicable is put in place in light of the existing circumstances.

NOW, THEREFORE BE IT RESOLVED by the Board of Directors of the Brazos River Authority that it would not oppose policy that would contemplate the sale of Brazos River Authority leased lots for the fair market value of the unencumbered fee simple estate less an offset of not more than ten percent (10 percent) of that value in recognition of the value of the leasehold interest.

The aforementioned resolution was approved by the Board of Directors of the Brazos River Authority on April 27, 2007, to certify which witness my hand and seal.

Roberto Bailon

Assistant Presiding Officer

The vote on the resolution was nine yes and three no.[101] The three members who voted against the resolution were Roberto Bailon, P. J. Ellison, and Billy Wayne Moore. All three stated that they were opposed to a forced divestiture outright. The nine who voted *yes* were all convinced that it would be best to "stop the bleeding." This would be the last meeting held by the BRA board during the current legislative session.

Six days later, on May 4, Senator Estes took his newly acquired deal to the Senate in the form of a floor amendment to Senate Bill 1326.[102] He explained that an agreement had been reached as to the method for valuing the land and explained the 10 percent discount. When the vote was taken to approve the amendment, the tally was twenty-three yeas and five nays.[103] The five senators who voted no were Kip Averitt, Glenn Hegar, Robert Nichols, Steve Ogden, and Dan Patrick.

---

101 Directors Adams, Baker, Butler, Garcia, Hughes, Martin, and Pena were absent. Wade Gear had already left to go to a client meeting.

102 Sen. Craig Estes, "Senate Session," Senate RealMedia Video Archives, 3:08:45, Texas Senate, May 4, 2007, accessed July 20, 2013. http://www.senate.state.tx.us/avarchive/ramav.php?ram=00003415.

103 "Senate Journal," Eighty-First Legislature—Regular Session, Texas Senate, May 4, 2007, p. 1715. http://www.journals.senate.state.tx.us/sjrnl/80r/pdf/80RSJ05-04-F. PDF#page=25.

Senator Estes then moved that the floor amendment be sent to engrossment. To which Lt. Governor David Dewhurst, who was presiding over the Senate, replied, "You're smiling too much. You're giving yourself away."[104]

That odd comment was actually an inside joke. Lt. Governor Dewhurst had been instrumental in helping Senator Estes ram the forced compromise down the BRA's throat.

At this point, there were twenty-four days left in the Eightieth Regular Session of the Texas legislature, and Senate Bill 1326 had the inertia that it needed to pass. The only hurdle left was to get past the Natural Resources Committee in the House.

104 Lt. Gov. David Dewhurst, "Senate Session," Senate RealMedia Video Archives, 3:23:19, Texas Senate, May 4, 2007, accessed July 20, 2013. http://www.senate.state.tx.us/avarchive/ramav.php?ram=00003415.

Chapter 10

THINK LONG, THINK WRONG

There's an old saying in poker that goes like this: "If you think long, you think wrong." This is especially true if you are feeling greedy and trying to press your luck.

About two weeks after Senator Estes had closed his handshake deal on the 90 percent agreement, Senate Bill 1326 went before the House Committee on Natural Resources on May 16, 2007.[105] Representative Jim Keffer offered his usual rambling explanation of the bill and stated multiple times that the issue was contentious and emotional. Inexplicably, Keffer then explained that a committee substitute was being offered that removed the 90 percent agreement that established the value of the property at the unencumbered fee simple estate, less a 10 percent offset.

Evidently, during the twelve days since Senator Estes had amended Senate Bill 1326 to include the agreement to sell the property at 90 percent of its fair market value, someone had gotten greedy and decided that there

105 Rep. Jim Keffer, "House Natural Resources Committee," Texas House of Representatives Broadcast Archives, 47:10, Texas House of Representatives, May 16, 2007, accessed July 24, 2013. rtsp://realvideoe.house.state.tx.us:554/archives/cmte80r/70516a30.rm.

was a better deal to be had. It would seem that Matt Phillips was correct when he said, "Trust me. They want 30 [percent]."

There were two freshmen from the Republican Party serving on the Natural Resources Committee that day, Representatives Mike O'Day and Brandon Creighton. When Brandon Creighton attempted to ask the first question to clarify the absence of the 90 percent agreement, Jim Keffer looked at the committee chairman and joked, "You let freshmen ask questions?"[106]

As it turns out, they do. Senate Bill 1326 was walking into a freshman buzz saw.

The first witness to take the podium in favor of SB 1326 was Mr. Robert Aldrich, who identified himself as a lawyer and a representative of the Possum Kingdom Lake Preservation Association.[107] Lance Byrd was still leading the charge from the back of the room, and Robert Aldrich was steering the boat toward Niagara Falls. Aldrich testified for right at thirty minutes, and the results were disastrous.

Robert Aldrich spent the first thirteen minutes attempting to explain who owned what, who had spent what, and why the leaseholders should be allowed to purchase their property at well below the fair market value of the unencumbered fee simple estate. He also attempted to explain a formula for discounting the property for the value of the leases that would disappear the second that the properties were sold. He also went to great lengths to convince the committee that the annual lease rates that the Possum Kingdom lessees were paying were not below market.

No one followed Aldrich's arguments, so freshman Mike O'Day attempted to ask some specific questions.[108] His line of inquiry focused on establishing who would own the lakefront houses upon the termination of

---

106 Rep. Jim Keffer, "House Natural Resources Committee," Texas House of Representatives Broadcast Archives, 50:16, Texas House of Representatives, May 16, 2007, accessed July 24, 2013. rtsp://realvideoe.house.state.tx.us:554/archives/cmte80r/70516a30.rm.

107 Robert Aldrich, "House Natural Resources Committee," Texas House of Representatives Broadcast Archives, 53:47, Texas House of Representatives, May 16, 2007, accessed July 24, 2013. rtsp://realvideoe.house.state.tx.us:554/archives/cmte80r/70516a30.rm.

108 Rep. Mike O'Day, "House Natural Resources Committee," Texas House of Representatives Broadcast Archives, 1:07:40, Texas House of Representatives, May 16, 2007, accessed July 24, 2013. rtsp://realvideoe.house.state.tx.us:554/archives/cmte80r/70516a30.rm.

the individual leases and establishing the fact that the annual rental fees on the lakefront property were substantially below market.

> **O'Day:** Let me see if I understand your process. What you are saying is the value of the land would be established by what the future value of the land would be at the termination of the lease in today's dollars, less the future value of the lease.

> **Aldrich:** Well, uh, yes. There is a factor by which the land will increase over the remaining term of the lease. It will appreciate some. That appreciation is calculated over the twenty years, let's say, in my example, and then there is a discount rate applied to that. What you do is you just net it out of the discount rate, and so there's a, it's normally around 8 percent. You take an 8 percent discount rate on the rent, discount that back, and then, say you had a 2 percent over the life increase, or 2 percent a year, which is the same as 8 percent a year. I mean that's the way the discount rate is going backwards, like interest. Then you have a 6, you discount it at 6 percent as opposed to 8 percent.

Is it any wonder that this guy couldn't close the deal?

> **O'Day:** How do you establish what that future value is of the land?

> **Aldrich:** The appraisers can do that. I mean, they have to establish the fair market value of the dirt today. Now we're just talking about the dirt; we're not talking about the structures. And then they can say, based on, whatever they base it on, they say this land during this period will appreciate X percent. And they do that. Fundamentally, that's one of the considerations that any licensed, knowledgeable appraiser would take into account.

In other words, Aldrich wanted the appraisers to ignore the fact that the BRA would own the lakefront homes that the leaseholders had built, upon the termination of the individual leases. Mike O'Day was not buying it.

> **O'Day:** Normal leases, you know, if you normally lease a piece of land, any improvements that aren't mobile become part of the land to the lessor. How is your lease structured?

Aldrich: The lease is silent as to that. And the law is both ways. There are cases that say that if it's silent to it, the structures go back to the, go to the lessor at the end of the term. In this case the BRA has said, "We know, you know, that y'all built that."

And in their promulgated or proposed lease it said, you know, if the lease goes back to us, if it's terminated at some point or when it's terminated, that you can take your structure with you.

O'Day: I haven't seen these homes, but I understand there's some pretty nice houses out there. It would be pretty tough to take one along with you.

Aldrich: It would be tough to take a house. Obviously, if it was a trailer house, and the tires aren't too bad on it, you could take it with you.

O'Day: I haven't had a whole lot of time to get involved in this. But I understand that these leases that you have now that are relatively inexpensive have sold for some pretty big dollars for the ability to be able to use that land for the next eighteen years or whatever that is.

Aldrich: Well, thirty years is what the normal term of the lease is. And the BRA historically, when somebody has bought and asked for a new lease, they've gotten a new lease.

O'Day: So they have been good neighbors.

Aldrich: Yeah, over time. Listen, as far as I, I mean there hadn't been until these last few years, I mean, it's been, I'll say, peaceful coexistence.

O'Day: It was a pretty sweet deal. Any time you can buy—or rent, rather—a lakefront lot, you know, for seventy dollars a month is a pretty good deal.

Aldrich: Well it's the same anywhere. Because—

O'Day: *Not in my part of the world, you can't rent a lakefront lot for seventy bucks!*

Representative O'Day had a point. About forty-five days prior to this hearing, Governor Rick Perry had sold a half acre of lakefront property on Lake LBJ for $1.15 million. Robert Aldrich stammered around a few more seconds until Representative Mike O'Day finally just said, "Okay, thank you," with more than a modicum of disgust in his voice.

The next committee member to question Robert Aldrich was Representative Dan Gattis, who was an attorney and rancher in Jonah, Texas.[109] Representative Gattis got straight to the point by accusing the leaseholders of attempting to legislate a land-grab before the rental rates were increased from seventy dollars per month to rates that were based upon the fair market value.

> **Gattis:** My concern is, my concern on this whole issue is, that we are not, we haven't taken into consideration, um, the fact that the lease rate can be renegotiated. And I see this move more as a way to try to get the property before that can be renegotiated because of the increase in the value that will be affected by the renegotiation of the lease.
>
> And what we are basically asking the BRA to do is sell a piece of property for less than what its true market value is. Which lease rate do we use as to what the value of the property is? The value of the current lease? Or the value of those leases that have been flipped out in the open market? Shouldn't that be the value that would really make a determination?
>
> **Aldrich:** No, because if you do that, Representative Gattis, you then take away the value that the lessees have paid. That's what I was talking about when I was going through the history. If you just value the lease, and say okay, it's worth $200,000 because somebody paid that for one right down the road. That $200,000 that was paid was not paid to the BRA, but it was paid to a former lessee.
>
> **Gattis:** Well, in the renegotiations standpoint, from the BRA's standpoint of what the value of these leases are, shouldn't that be taken into consideration? Of what these things are flipping for out there in the open market?
>
> **Aldrich:** No.
>
> **Gattis:** *Why not?*
>
> **Aldrich:** Why not is because that's not part of the formula.
>
> **Gattis:** I am not asking about the formula as to the price paid for it if you decide to purchase the property. I am asking in the

---

109 Rep. Dan Gattis, "House Natural Resources Committee," Texas House of Representatives Broadcast Archives, 1:15:28, Texas House of Representatives, May 16, 2007, accessed July 24, 2013. rtsp://realvideoe.house.state.tx.us:554/archives/cmte80r/70516a30.rm.

renegotiation issue of the lease that they get to do every five years. Shouldn't that be taken into consideration of what the market value truly is of that lease?

Aldrich: Well, okay. I think I understand what you're asking. You're talking about in those five-year windows where they can raise the lease rates.

Gattis: Yes, sir.

Aldrich: They don't renegotiate the leases; they just can raise the lease rates. Okay, I see what you're saying. The BRA, it certainly as the owner, as the lessor, it can do whatever it wants with those lease rates every five years.

What prudent lessors do is look around and say, okay, what, what am I really asking? What are these lessees really paying? And that goes back to my example about, we're not really underpaying anything because we're paying a thousand, fifteen hundred, two thousand—whatever it is a year. Plus, we're paying the ad valorem taxes that the BRA is exempt from paying. If the BRA had to pay the taxes why, yeah, we'd sure have to pay them the taxes, because they're the lessor.

So do you take that into consideration? I would assume an appraiser would take the, the, the only way I know an appraiser can do it is to historically go back and say, "Okay, here is what has happened. Here is what happened with the land, and here is what has happened with the lease payments."

And they can come up with a factor to adjust that with. And if that's the way an appraiser does it, based on what the case law says he or she has to do, then so be it. I mean that's fine.

After about five seconds, Representative Dan Gattis replied, "Okay. Thank you, sir," and yielded the floor. Aldrich did not seem to realize that he was making it clear that everyone was making money off the BRA's property except for the BRA and the taxpayers of Texas.

Representative Brandon Creighton took the floor next.[110] When he wasn't serving in the Texas legislature, he practiced as an attorney and as

110 Rep. Brandon Creighton, "House Natural Resources Committee," Texas House of Representatives Broadcast Archives, 1:18:43, Texas House of Representatives, May 16, 2007, accessed July 24, 2013. rtsp://realvideoe.house.state.tx.us:554/archives/cmte80r/70516a30.rm.

a real estate developer in Conroe. As such, it would appear that he had a fairly strong grasp of the nature and structure of leaseholds. Representative Creighton proceeded to take Robert Aldrich to school on the folly of building extremely expensive homes on property that one does not own. He then effectively accused Aldrich and the other leaseholders of betting on the come and expecting the legislature to make sure that they did not crap out.

> **Creighton:** Mr. Aldrich, how long have you been a lessee?
>
> **Aldrich:** Well, I've been a lessee this time, for about eleven years, ten and a half years. My father first got a lease out there in '57, so I've been around that lake since I was five years old. I know I look older than that, but …
>
> **Creighton:** So when you received or you negotiated for that leasehold interest, did you have a purchase option in your lease or a lease-purchase provision?
>
> **Aldrich:** No, sir.
>
> **Creighton:** So you did not have any expectation of purchasing the property or getting the value or recovering the value, of putting money into improvements or paying taxes or anything associated with putting—
>
> **Aldrich:** *Sure, I did!*
>
> **Creighton:** Even though—you did, even though you didn't have the expectation of purchasing the land?
>
> **Aldrich:** Sure! Sure! That's right!

Well, in the back of my mind has always been at some point the BRA is going to want to be out of here, because other lakes have gone the same way over the years. So I thought, okay, fine. We'll come to that.

Did I know, for a fact, that maybe someday I would be able to buy my lease lot? No. Did it make any difference to me in 1996? No. Because the history of the BRA for sixty years at that point had been to have reasonable leases, with reasonable lease rates, and always extend the lease. That's its history.

So anybody coming out there, they're going to come into the same position. When I say the BRA, there was a sea change in the early 2000s. There was clearly a sea change in how it addressed these leases.

Creighton: There was a sea change, but in the original agreement, there was no discussion of an option to purchase or for recovering any kind of value for money put into the property or the leasehold estate.

Aldrich: Well, part A to your question is, there was absolutely no purchase option in my lease or anybody else's that I've ever heard of.

Part B is what I recover, what I put into the place. *Yes!* If I wanted to sell, then based on the BRA's practices for sixty years, I could sell that lease. And I could get my money out of the lease.

That changed! Last year.

Creighton: So there are, you know, common practices, for what a prudent lessor, the way a prudent lessor may carry their business, but in the end, it is up to the lessor as far as the amount that they ask for the value of what they own.

Aldrich: That's right. The lessor can do it. It can be a prudent lessor, an imprudent lessor—it can be any kind of lessor that it wants. Now that is not without the possibility of penalty. But it can certainly do that. Yes, sir.

Evidently, Representative Dan Gattis had heard enough at this point. He quietly rose from his seat and left the committee room.

Creighton: And when you leased this property, you had in mind that years and years from that time, because there was precedent with other river authorities and lakes, you know, conveying or assigning or transferring their interests in this same manner, that one day, you would be able to possibly do the same thing, and then here we are today?

Aldrich: No. I wouldn't even say that that was in my mind. What I said was, I knew, I mean I've been around Possum Kingdom for years. I just, I figured at some point the BRA would not want to lease lots anymore. That's as far as it went.

Creighton: That was a pretty good hunch.

Aldrich: If you're asking me what my mind-set was. My mind-set was when I bought my place was not that I was going to buy the place. My mind-set was, I've been around here a lot of years. I know what the BRA does. It's a fair deal. I'm not going to lose money because it's a lease. You know that's scares lots of people away.

Creighton: Mr. Aldrich, thank you.

The only thing that spared Robert Aldrich from himself and more damaging testimony was a point of order related to time that prevented anymore questions. We will never know if the committee members present that day would have approved the deal that required a fair market appraisal of the fee simple estate and provided for a 10 percent offset. What we do know is that Senator Craig Estes and Representative Jim Keffer would not make the mistake of allowing their charitable piece of legislation to cross paths with these gentlemen again in the future.

The committee was recessed and would reconvene later that day to hear testimony from the opposing side. At the beginning of the evening session, it was announced that the committee substitute had been withdrawn and that the 90 percent deal was back on the table. Unfortunately for the leaseholders, the damage had already been done.

Representatives Gattis and Creighton were not present for the opposing testimony that evening. Perhaps they had already made up their minds as to the merits of SB 1326. The first to speak was Carolyn Johnson.[111] As her testimony began, Representative Mike Hamilton, the vice-chairman of the Natural Resources Committee, left the meeting. There was no longer a quorum present and thus, no action could be taken other than testimony.

Carolyn Johnson stated that she was opposed to selling the BRA's lakefront property in general and believed that the BRA had acted responsibly in voting to increase annual rental rates to market value. This was done, she stressed, to ensure that the BRA's water customers "do not have to compensate for PK lessees paying bargain-basement rates." True to form, Carolyn summed up her position candidly.

> It is my firm belief that the actions by former BRA boards led to an entitlement feeling from the lessees for low lease rates. This entitlement mentality that has developed among our lessees has

111 Carolyn Johnson, "House Natural Resources Committee," Texas House of Representatives Broadcast Archives, 5:52, Texas House of Representatives, May 16, 2007, accessed July 24, 2013. rtsp://realvideoe.house.state.tx.us:554/archives/cmte80r/70516p30.rm.

resulted in this massive controversy and contentious situation we're in today.[112]

The next to speak was Roberto "Bob" Bailon, who served as the assistant presiding officer of the BRA's Board. Bob stated that the board was attempting to serve the best interests of the eleven million Texans who lived in the Brazos River Basin. In an angry tone, he characterized SB 1326 in the following manner.

> The asset of a properly functioning body is being essentially confiscated and put up for sale, to private individuals I might add. This is terribly bad policy, public policy. It abrogates our responsibilities. It circumvents state law that prohibits the sale of property directly to individuals and so forth. And it causes a significant financial impact on the entire basin.[113]

The next to speak was Wade Gear. As I mentioned earlier, there are usually two sides to every story, and Robert Aldrich had already offered the perspective of the leaseholders. For the next eight minutes, Wade Gear would offer what was arguably the seminal statement by a conscientious public servant concerning the forced divestiture of property at Possum Kingdom Lake.

> Mr. Chairman, members, my name is Wade Gear. I'm a member of the Brazos River Authority board of directors. I'm here to testify in opposition to Senate Bill 1326. I have been involved with Possum Kingdom Lake for many years, both as a property owner and as a member of the board of directors.

> Upon my appointment to the board several years ago, I was very critical and outspoken in regards to the way the Authority was handling issues at Possum Kingdom, specifically the lessees. After studying the facts, and really evaluating what was occurring at

---

112 Carolyn Johnson, "House Natural Resources Committee," Texas House of Representatives Broadcast Archives, 9:00, Texas House of Representatives, May 16, 2007, accessed July 26, 2013. rtsp://realvideoe.house.state.tx.us:554/archives/cmte80r/70516p30.rm.

113 Roberto Bailon, "House Natural Resources Committee," Texas House of Representatives Broadcast Archives, 9:28, Texas House of Representatives, May 16, 2007, accessed July 26, 2013. rtsp://realvideoe.house.state.tx.us:554/archives/cmte80r/70516p30.rm.

PK, it became apparent to me that the BRA needed to admit that the problems at Possum Kingdom are a by-product of years of neglect. And while the lessees did not need to be overwhelmed with sweeping change, change was certainly necessary.

As chairman of the lake committee, I set a goal that we would be fair and reasonable in our decision-making process and the changes that we made. And I can tell you that we met our goal. And I firmly believe that the decisions of the board have been conservative and compassionate to all those at the lake. We have made good, sound business decisions, based on facts.

These facts have been collected over years by outside, disinterested real estate professionals. While these studies have been criticized, the fact remains that there is no supporting research, study, or data that contradicts these findings. In fact, I've made written requests of the chairman of the Possum Kingdom Lake Preservation Association, asking for any information supporting their statements and their views, and I have received no response.[114]

In other words, poor old Wade had to send a letter to his wife's uncle to discuss the matter instead of simply picking up the phone and asking, "What the hell are we doing here?" Wade Gear continued:

I've asked Mr. Aldrich, who testified earlier today, to provide this information as well. I've received nothing. In my opinion, the Possum Kingdom Lake Preservation Association wants to continue receiving discounts at the expense of the rest of our basin.

It's my understanding that the purpose of Senator Estes' bill is to get the BRA out of the land management business so that we can focus on the development of our water resources to meet the growing population of this state. Under this bill, we are faced with selling our single greatest appreciating asset at a discount. Unfortunately, what we know is that this bill will not get us out of the property management business. In fact, it will leave us with a patchwork of properties that we have to manage and that are owned by another party.

---

114 Wade Gear, "House Natural Resources Committee," Texas House of Representatives Broadcast Archives, 15:20, Texas House of Representatives, May 16, 2007, accessed July 26, 2013. rtsp://realvideoe.house.state.tx.us:554/archives/cmte80r/70516p30.rm.

In fact, I've even heard that there was a push to take the Section G out of this bill altogether, which perpetuates the hardship on the BRA and nullifies the original intent of this bill. This fact alone clearly illustrates that not everyone wants to buy their land at Possum Kingdom.

With over twenty years experience in real estate management, specifically managing income-producing assets of third parties, I can tell you that our responsibilities at the lake will not decrease proportionately with the sale of property. And in fact, I believe that we will find it more difficult to enforce two separate standards— one for owners and one for lessees—as well as the standards that are designed to protect the water quality for our customers downstream. From my perspective, the real losers will be the people who depend upon us now and in the future for their water.

Let me give you some facts. Current county tax records reflect that the BRA has $101 million of assets under lease at Possum Kingdom. Our revenues are less than $1.5 million, which is less than a 1.5 percent return, and that's before expenses.

Our average lease rate is $800 a year, or $67 a month, and lessees have historically been exempt from paying dock fees or water-usage fees. In comparison, the average twenty-five-foot boat slip in a marina at the lake leases for over $2,000 a year. I pay almost $3,000 a year for a boat slip in a marina.

A BRA commercial subleasing operation, which is included in this bill, it's called Sandbar Getaway, it's forty-four acres, it pays us $13,000 a year for forty-four acres. It has been subleased to approximately one hundred trailer-sized lots, and they pay up to $2,500 a year for these trailer-sized lots. Our lots are half an acre to three-fourths an acre, and upwards of two acres in some places, and our fees are called too high?

And here is a statistic that I'd like you to remember. There are 437,000 households that depend on the BRA for drinking water through their local municipalities that will be negatively impacted by this legislation. There are only 1,579 residential lessees, and for 84 percent of these people it represents their vacation or second homes.

Bottom line: this is not a local bill; this is a special-interest bill. It will serve the wants of a few wealthy individuals at the expense of the BRA and the entities whom we provide water.

It should serve as no surprise that the lessees moved to push this sale as soon as the board adopted a new market rate. They saw the sweet deal was coming to an end. The lessees have had the luxury of living at Possum Kingdom Lake for years and paying almost nothing. So why should they be allowed to benefit again by forcing the sale of the land below its actual worth? Again, remember that most of the lessees don't even live at the lake. These are their second homes.

I ask you that if you consider the sale of BRA land, at the very least the language should allow the BRA to sell the land for unencumbered fee simple value. And we should be allowed to get out of the land management business. However, that brings up an interesting point.

Our FERC license requires, and this is one of the issues that, while we've be so focused on the fair market value, we haven't looked at the fact that FERC guides us at the lake. FERC requires us to maintain public use facilities. There are also homes that are encroached within the FERC boundary that we have not approached FERC officially, because we don't know what bill to take FERC. But we don't know. FERC may not allow us to even sell those homes that are encroached, and some of them are specifically within the boundary completely.

Personally, and this is my litmus test, if I were entrusted with this asset for my own children's future, I would never sell it. It's a bad business decision. And in my opinion, it's bad policy. Thank you for your time.[115]

And with those comments, Wade Gear ensured that his days on the board of the Brazos River Authority were limited. He served at the pleasure of the governor, and the governor would not be pleased with his comments.

The next to speak was Steve Pena, who served as the presiding officer of the Brazos River Authority's board. Mr. Pena was also a certified public account from the Austin area. He spoke for over seven minutes, citing numerous statistics and valuations. His summation was direct.

---

115 Wade Gear, "House Natural Resources Committee," Texas House of Representatives Broadcast Archives, 15:20, Texas House of Representatives, May 16, 2007, accessed July 26, 2013. rtsp://realvideoe.house.state.tx.us:554/archives/cmte80r/70516p30.rm.

As you have heard before, the Brazos River Authority currently grosses $1.27 million per year on leases. This revenue is based on lease rates that are grossly under market.

So much so as I'd like to give you some statistics, if I could. Here's some examples of some of the other public lands that lease their lands out. The University Lands Division of the University of Texas targets 10 percent. The General Land Office targets 10 percent. The LCRA targets 10 to 12 percent and the US Corps of Engineers targets 10 percent. We've been limping along with 1.27 percent for too long. [...]

I urge you all to consider this bill very carefully and the impact that it will have not only on the Brazos River Authority but other similarly situated agencies in Texas.[116]

At the end of Mr. Pena's remarks, Representative Mike O'Day posed a few questions.[117]

O'Day: I'll ask a quick question, and I'd like a quick answer. Who maintains the shoreline currently?

Pena: The Brazos River Authority.

O'Day: How would that change if the property were sold?

Pena: I'm not sure.

O'Day: What advantage would there be for the Brazos River Authority to sell this property to the basin? What advantage to the basin would it be for the Brazos River Authority to sell this property?

Pena: None whatsoever that I can find.

O'Day and Pena exchanged a thank-you and this concluded the testimony of those in opposition to Senate Bill 1326. At this point,

---

116 Steve Pena, "House Natural Resources Committee," Texas House of Representatives Broadcast Archives, 22:14, Texas House of Representatives, May 16, 2007, accessed July 27, 2013. rtsp://realvideoe.house.state.tx.us:554/archives/cmte80r/70516p30.rm.

117 Rep. Mike O'Day, "House Natural Resources Committee," Texas House of Representatives Broadcast Archives, 29:00, Texas House of Representatives, May 16, 2007, accessed July 27, 2013. rtsp://realvideoe.house.state.tx.us:554/archives/cmte80r/70516p30.rm.

Representative Harvey Hilderbran left the meeting, leaving only three committee members present.

The last rule that I am going to bore you with is the Rule of Holes. This rule states:

> When you are in a hole, stop digging.

The leaseholders testifying that day did not seem to understand the Rule of Holes. Even though there was no quorum present, they continued to burden the record with their twisted logic. The first to do so was none other than the driving force behind divestiture, Mr. Lance Byrd.

> Yes, sir, I'm Lance Byrd. I'm a leaseholder at Possum Kingdom Lake. It's also my homestead. I'd like to testify that lots of us have made significant investments out there on these properties. We've paid to buy the right to lease the property at a significant cost. We paid for all the improvements. We paid for the water system.
>
> Everybody out there is not wealthy. Uh, neighbors are painters, retired teachers. We would just like the opportunity to buy our lots. And we're willing to pay the fair market value for it. As Mr. Pena said, this is the current compromise we've reached with the BRA on this, and this time we'd just like for them to honor it and accept it, and let's move forward, and allow us to buy these lots at fair market value.[118]

Lance Byrd turned to his left and had taken a step away from the podium when Representative Mike O'Day cleared his throat and asked for the floor. Lance Byrd stepped back in front of the microphone—and directly into O'Day's crosshairs. Representative O'Day was none too happy that the leaseholders had wasted the committee's time by withdrawing and then reinserting the 90 percent deal, and he let Lance Byrd know it.

> **O'Day:** Mr. Byrd, when you bought your lease, what did you pay for it?

---

118 Lance Byrd, "House Natural Resources Committee," Texas House of Representatives Broadcast Archives, 31:52, Texas House of Representatives, May 16, 2007, accessed July 27, 2013. rtsp://realvideoe.house.state.tx.us:554/archives/cmte80r/70516p30.rm.

Byrd: A hundred and fifty-five thousand dollars.

O'Day: And what was your expectation when your lease ran out?

Byrd: Well. I did a lot of due diligence. And I know the question in a lot of your minds is, "What kind of an idiot would build a house or put their homestead on land that they didn't own?"

Bingo.

Byrd: But I did a lot of due diligence. I talked to bankers. I talked to lease owners. I talked to employees of the BRA, and I got the same answer over and over. It's been like this for sixty-five years; it's not going to change; there's going to be nothing dramatic changing about it. I asked the BRA employee if I could have a new thirty-year lease when I bought this one, because it was already about ten years into it. "No problem; you fill out this form; you pay ten dollars."

I did it and got my lease. Everybody that I talked to—the banks, those at the BRA, the leaseholders—everybody said that it was going to continue this way.

O'Day: I'm missing the point here, because from what I'm hearing from the BRA, they want to continue things as they had it. What I'm hearing from your guys is that y'all want to force them into a sale. That didn't work exactly like you wanted, and now you want to back up and pick up the second part of being able to buy your property. So which is it? Do you want to stay where you are and have your lease, or do you want to buy the property?

Byrd: Well, the change they made to the lease, debate all you want whether eight hundred dollars a year is fair or not, that's the rules they made. That's the rules they presented us, and we accepted those and that's what we went forward with. The changes they're suggesting are exponentially changing that. My lot, for example, the projections that they have tied to the increases in appraisal rates with the Palo Pinto tax district—I could pay over the period of a fifty-year lease $750,000 in lease payments for this now, as opposed to what was a reasonable amount before.

O'Day: I've never been to Possum Kingdom, and I hear it's a really fantastic place, but in Houston, if you lived in a nice subdivision, your homeowners association dues, just to do the common areas, would be more expensive than what you're paying for your lease for your land.

Byrd: And I think that's what needs to happen. There needs to be a homeowners association that manages us. We need to govern ourselves. But not be under the management of a river authority that's spending these dollars. And that's another thing. This is a huge windfall for the River Authority. It's a good deal for them. I'm surprised they're fighting it. It's a good deal for them. Millions of dollars will come into their coffers.

Representative O'Day cut him off, raising his voice.

O'Day: Well, it probably was a good deal, and they agreed to the last proposal that you had, and then there was an amendment that was brought up that canceled that deal. So now we're backing up again.

Byrd: I didn't ask to have it put in. I am in favor of Senator Estes' bill as is, as it passed the Senate.

O'Day: Okay, thank you.

Again Lance Byrd tried to escape from the podium, and again he was called back by Chairman Puente. This time it was Representative Jodie Laubenberg who posed the only question that she would ask during the entire divestiture process.

If the name Jodie Laubenberg sounds familiar, it should. This same state representative, who has represented the Eighty-Ninth District of Texas since 2003, was also the House sponsor of the now infamous Senate Bill 5 that was introduced on June 11, 2013.[119] This occurred during the first special session called by Governor Rick Perry, which ended in the eleven-hour filibuster by Senator Wendy Davis, which propelled her into the national spotlight. Over the course of a few hours, Senator Davis went from a few hundred Twitter followers to over one hundred thousand. In response to that response, Senator Davis decided to run for governor of the state of Texas.

---

119 Depending on your point of view, the term *famous* might be equally appropriate.

When asked about the prudence of denying a woman access to an abortion subsequent to a rape event, Representative Jodie Laubenberg declared the scenario irrelevant. Her explanation was that when a woman gets raped, she goes to the local hospital, where a rape kit is administered. She further explained that these kits "clean you out," and you will not get pregnant. Thus, the issue of rape is a nonissue.[120] I can't help but think that her comments regarding rape kits gave the tied-up goats in the state of Texas a strong sense of relief.

> **Laubenberg:** When you said you're willing to pay the fair market value, is that with the encumbered, uh, or unencumbered?

Wow. Was that a blistering line of questioning or what?

> **Byrd:** I don't like that. But we've got to do something. We can't continue under this proposal that they have. I don't like it. But I'll accept it.

This answer drew Representative O'Day back into the conversation.

> **O'Day:** One more question. In one of the things that was described here, the homeowners would have an opportunity to buy certain pieces. Is there anything in y'all's agreement or in the negotiations to be able to buy them out completely, so that if we want to take the BRA out of the land business, is somebody else willing to come in there and buy all of the lots so that they don't have to be in the land business? Or do we just get to pick and choose? Do the residents get to pick and choose which lots they would like to have out of the lease?
>
> **Byrd:** Well, at this point, we're just asking for us to have the opportunity for the individual lessees to buy our own lots.
>
> **O'Day:** Okay. And what do they do with the balance of that?
>
> **Byrd:** I'd say at that point that's a management decision on their part. Uh, if they want to sell them.

---

120 Nick Wing, "Jodie Laubenberg, Texas GOP Lawmaker, Suggests Rape Kits Can Give Abortions," *Huffington Post*, June 24, 2013, accessed November 1, 2013. http://www.huffingtonpost.com/2013/06/24/jodie-laubenberg-texas-rape_n_3493220.html.

O'Day: Is it not a management decision on their part right now as to what they're doing? What's the difference in where you are putting them and where they are?

Byrd: I'm sorry; I don't understand your question.

O'Day: Well, if you're saying that they have the lots left over and it's their job to do something with the lots, they've either got to lease the lots or they've got to sell the lots, if they have no buyers for the lots except for the people—

Byrd: I would suggest that there would be a very small percentage of people that don't exercise the opportunity to buy their lots.

O'Day: Well, I guess we need to hear from the larger percentage because from what I've heard, it's about a 50–50 deal.

Byrd: I haven't heard any lease owners testify here today that weren't in favor of buying their lots, and I haven't talked to any that weren't in favor of buying their lots.

O'Day: Well, we've only heard from three, so it's pretty hard to judge that.

Byrd: But none of them are here to say that they're not interested in buying their lots.

Lance Byrd was finally excused from the podium and was replaced by Jay Turner. Turner spoke only briefly and, as usual, tried to convince anyone who would listen that he was seeking nothing more than a mutually beneficial outcome.

Thank you, Mr. Chairman and members of the committee. My name is Jay Turner. I've been a leaseholder at Possum Kingdom since 1989. I've been visiting that lake since 1965. I've been very involved in this process since it began a couple of years ago, trying to obtain a fair and mutually beneficial solution for both sides. And now we're here today, at this eleventh hour.

The bill that's in front of you right now is the very bill that the BRA agreed to in the Senate version. That's what they had agreed to. As Mr. Byrd said, we're not particularly that fond of it, but we need a bill out of this session of the legislature, and that's the one that we would agree to accept. There's some of the language in there we don't like, but again, we would agree to accept that.

It's been alluded to by several of the speakers from the board for the BRA of the sweet deal, the below-market rates, and so forth and so on. The fact is this process has taken sixty-five years to get here. And every lessee that has signed a lease has done exactly what the BRA has promulgated and proposed and told us to do. And the financial decisions that were made by every purchaser of a property there were made under those rules. And the BRA determined that because they're losing money, I guess, that they need to raise those rates. And a lot of the lessees said okay, you can raise those rates.

I became involved when initially they said we're going to look at the market value or the tax-appraised value of that property, of the land, on the tax rolls and apply a rate to that. And initially it was 6 percent. And that 6 percent lease rate was very difficult for a lot of people. There are some very nice homes at Possum Kingdom Lake, but a lot of those homes are already on deeded property. There are a lot of homes out there that are second- and third-generation homes with retired folks, with people on fixed income, with elderly people.

I know Mr. Gear said 84 percent are second homes. I don't know where that number came from. I'm not going to stand here and dispute it, because I don't know. But I do know that there are a lot of homes out there that if you drove around and looked at them, you wouldn't say, "This is an affluent property."

The fact is every lessee has done exactly what the BRA has said. Recently the Palo Pinto appraisal district has been sending out reappraisals of property. I talked to a seventy-one-year-old gentleman that has .62 acres of property, a little over a half an acre. It was on the tax roll on the land for about $65,000. It jumped to $191,900 for the land only for .62 acres. So this gentleman, in his retirement years, is looking at a lease payment based on $191,900, plus whatever the improvements are, plus the property taxes that he has to pay. So a lot of those people will be displaced.[121]

---

121 Jay Turner, "House Natural Resources Committee," Texas House of Representatives Broadcast Archives, 38:29, Texas House of Representatives, May 16, 2007, accessed July 27, 2013. rtsp://realvideoe.house.state.tx.us:554/archives/cmte80r/70516p30.rm.

What Jay Turner actually accomplished was to remind everyone that the only reason that he was involved was because the rent on his lakefront property would soon be tied to market rates.

Perhaps the most damaging testimony offered that day came from Dennis Cannedy, who was the final witness to testify in favor of Senate Bill 1326.

> Thank you, Mr. Chair. My name is Dennis Cannedy, and I'm a leaseholder down at PK, and I'm a CPA with about thirty years in private practice. What I would like to do today, let's kind of talk numbers and where this thing may go, could go, or should go.[122]

Dennis Cannedy obviously did not realize that Senate Bill 1326 wasn't going anywhere in the absence of a quorum. He also did not seem to realize that the 90 percent deal had been put back on the table.

Perhaps what Cannedy should have said is, "Thank you, Mr. Chair. My name is Dennis Cannedy, and I am the campaign treasurer for Senator Estes, who is sponsoring this piece of bullshit pork." What Cannedy should not have done is provide a lengthy dissertation explaining that the BRA's valuation methodology would yield $200 million, while the methodology that the leaseholders were asking for would only yield $100 million. Both of these estimates would make the $50 million that the River Card paid for the property look absurd by comparison.

The final witness to testify before the House Natural Resources Committee on May 16, 2007, was Matt Phillips, who served as the manager of governmental affairs for the BRA. Phillips took the podium and, in so doing, put his job on the line.

> I'm Matt Phillips with the Brazos River Authority. I'll be real brief. There were a couple of things said that I just want to clarify.
>
> The idea of the 6 percent lease rate. I wanted to be real clear, because one thing that wasn't mentioned is that the rate does not get to 6 percent for twenty years. It takes twenty years to actually march up to 6 percent. So that's one thing.

---

122 Dennis Cannedy, "House Natural Resources Committee," Texas House of Representatives Broadcast Archives, 43:30, Texas House of Representatives, May 16, 2007, accessed July 28, 2013. rtsp://realvideoe.house.state.tx.us:554/archives/cmte80r/70516p30.rm.

Second, with regard to those who are over sixty-five and homesteaded, the board has considered doing discounts for them and at one time was going to consider completely freezing the rates for the sixty-five and older; however, had to stop that proposal because of the fact that the legislation could have allowed those freezes to further discount the property. So that was the reason that the board had to pull that proposal off the table.

Second of all, with regard to the Staubach study, and talking about encumbrances to title and selling land encumbered, those things apply in a willing buyer, willing seller transaction which this is *not*. The BRA is not a willing seller. We are being made to sell, directed to sell.

The last thing I'll say is there was some talk about $95 million, making $95 million. That's assuming everybody buys, which we would contest. Maybe 50 percent, probably less, if I had to guess. I mean, if you just financed a home, you'd be upside down if you tried to do that.

In addition, the idea of BRA trying to create some sort of windfall is *false*. All BRA is trying to do is ensure a break even in this transaction. Over the next twenty years, we can anticipate through the increasing of lease rates to make $80 million for the system. So that makes that ninety or so million dollars not look as big anymore. All we're trying to do is ensure is that the money that the BRA loses through pulling homes off of the lease rolls is fully made up by what we have to sell it for. So there is no windfall. It's a break even. And I'll be happy to answer any questions.[123]

While Matt Phillips's remarks were candid and honest, he was an employee who was on the state payroll, supporting board members who were appointed by the governor. And while he may have been conscientious, his positions were not consistent with that of the governor. As a result, he would soon be serving a bit of time in the penalty box.

At the end of the testimony, a defeated Jim Keffer walked to the podium to offer his closing remarks.

---

123 Matt Phillips, "House Natural Resources Committee," Texas House of Representatives Broadcast Archives, 52:04, Texas House of Representatives, May 16, 2007, accessed July 28, 2013. rtsp://realvideoe.house.state.tx.us:554/archives/cmte80r/70516p30.rm.

Well, thank you very much. And you can see some of the complexities that we have been going through these last few years, actually. But, uh, the Estes bill as filed, as you see there before you, is an agreed-to bill, now with the parties, and I would ask for your positive look, and, uh, movement on this bill.[124]

The chairman of the House Natural Resources Committee, Robert Puente, motioned to his left and then stated, "Mr. Keffer, there's …"

And then he stopped. He was indicating that there were only two other committee members left in the hearing room and that no action could be taken. Jim Keffer replied, "Yes, I see."

Chairman Puente then stated, "The Chair leaves Senate Bill 1326 pending."

And with that, Keffer walked off with his hands in his pockets. By all accounts, it appeared that Senate Bill 1326 would die a quiet death. The leaseholders had literally snatched defeat from the jaws of victory.

---

124 Rep. Jim Keffer, "House Natural Resources Committee," Texas House of Representatives Broadcast Archives, 31:52, Texas House of Representatives, May 16, 2007, accessed July 28, 2013. rtsp://realvideoe.house.state.tx.us:554/archives/cmte80r/70516p30.rm.

Chapter 11

THE HAIL MARY

On December 28, 1975, Roger Staubach squared off against fellow future Hall of Fame quarterback Fran Tarkenton in the NFC Divisional Playoff. With thirty-seven seconds remaining in the game, Staubach faced second down with ten yards to go. He was trailing by a score of 14 to 10, and the line of scrimmage was at midfield. And for that, he was fortunate. Two plays earlier, on fourth down with seventeen yards to go, Drew Pearson had made what might have been the most spectacular sideline catch of his Hall of Fame–worthy career.

What happened next is burned into the memory of every true Texan. Rather than trying to systematically move the ball down the field, Staubach called on Drew Pearson one more time to close the deal. The Cowboys set up in the shotgun formation that had been invented by the same man who had also invented the flex defense. That man was the legendary Tom Landry, who was known for twenty-eight years as "the only head coach that the Cowboys have ever had."

Before the snap, Roger looked to his left and then to his right. The snap was clean, and Roger halfheartedly pump-faked to the left side of the field. He then cocked his magic right arm and let go of what would almost immediately and forever be remembered as the "Hail Mary."

Drew Pearson worked a little magic of his own on the other end. Using what he calls a "swim move" and what All-Pro defensive back Nate Washington calls offensive pass interference, Pearson trapped the ball on his hip while Washington was lying prone on the ground. Drew Pearson literally waltzed into the end zone with the game-winning score.

What we are trying to determine here is whether selling $1 billion worth of real estate for $50 million was simply bureaucratic bungling at its finest or something more egregious—as in, something that violated the law. We still have a long way to go on that, but I can tell you this right now: The fact that Drew Pearson is not in the NFL Hall of Fame is an absolute crime. The man is being robbed of his proper legacy, not unlike Bob Hayes for so many years.

One thing that people tend to forget about the Hail Mary is that the Dallas Cowboys lost to the Pittsburgh Steelers two games later in Super Bowl IX.[125] While comparing Senator Craig Estes to Roger Staubach is nothing short of sacrilege, Estes was about to experience a very similar win-lose scenario.

On May 22, 2007, there were six days left in the Eightieth Legislative Session. The House of Representatives was meeting on the floor of the chamber, and the topic of the day was Senate Bill 3, an omnibus water bill. There were 101 amendments attached to Senate Bill 3 that day, and Senator Craig Estes was number 63 in line.

As Estes was a senator, and this was a session of the House of Representatives, he would need to increase his stable by one more player. He staked his bet on Representative Dan Branch from District 108 in Dallas. What followed next would later be referred to by Paul Burka of the *Texas Monthly* as a "dog and pony show."[126]

Representative Dan Branch offered the entirety of Senate Bill 1326, as approved by the Texas Senate as Amendment 63 to Senate Bill 3.

---

125 People also forget that the father of the legendary quarterback of the Minnesota Vikings, Fran Tarkenton, died tragically of a heart attack during the third quarter of that game. Ironically, the senior Tarkenton's first name was Dallas. Fran Tarkenton also went on to a successful career in business.

126 Paul Burka, "The Next Speaker," *Texas Monthly*, December 20, 2008, accessed March 1, 2010. http://www.texasmonthly.com/burka-blog/next-speaker.

Representative Dan Gattis, who had grilled leaseholder Robert Aldrich during the House Natural Resources Committee hearing, asked Dan Branch to yield for some questions. Gattis also asked that the conversation be recorded in the House Journal. The following is the official discussion between the two Representatives.

Tuesday, May 22, 2007 HOUSE JOURNAL 4987

Regular Session 81st Day

REMARKS ORDERED PRINTED—STATEMENT OF LEGISLATIVE INTENT

Gattis: Representative Branch, you understand that this was a bill that came through committee and never made it out of committee. You understand that? It came down through Natural Resources.

Branch: Yes.

Gattis: Several of us had some major concerns with this bill. But my understanding is that BRA and the property owners around here kind of negotiated an agreement, or a stalemate I guess may be the best way to put it.

And I think we are all okay with this, but I just want to get some intent to avoid some future problems in this issue. You are not aware of any law in the state of Texas that requires BRA to sell their property unless they want to—is that your understanding?

Branch: That's right. It was taken sixty-five years ago by eminent domain. And it was for use of the Brazos River and maintaining flood control; then the reservoir, as I understand. The dam will never be able to come fifteen feet higher.

So what turned out to be potentially excess flood control land has now turned into thirty-year lease property with mixed types of uses, from trailers to nice homes.

Gattis: And initially this was flood land. But because they couldn't raise the dam level, they lease this out for fishing shacks and those types of things. But now we have, on some of these leases, half-million-dollar homes. Is that your understanding?

Branch: That's my understanding; that's right.

Gattis: And there is no requirement that BRA sell this land to those people who have these homes on these leasehold estates. Is that correct?

Branch: Not to my knowledge.

Gattis: In fact, this bill that came through the legislature, that now you've added as an amendment, is what would allow BRA to sell this property, to sell these leasehold estates, sell the property actually to the people that have these homes, or these trailers, on this property. Is that your understanding?

Branch: That's right. And hopefully, the way I see it, it's a win-win. Not only for the River Authority, which affects, as you know, sixty-five counties and one of our major rivers. But also it will be good for the communities, and the school districts, and the municipalities, and the counties around Possum Kingdom Lake, and can attract more capital, more investment, and help out those communities.

Gattis: One of the disagreements throughout this process has continually been, what is the price if BRA decides to sell this property? What would be the price?

The current law is a little bit differing on what exactly that price would be. Some believe that you would have to consider the leasehold estate. BRA argues that you don't. That has been the contention that has walked us all the way through this process.

But what we have before us—your amendment and your amendment to the amendment, your amendment as amended—is the compromise that BRA has agreed to and these leasehold interests have agreed to and said, "All right, we will agree. Even though we don't have to, we will agree to this bill. We will agree to sell this property, but we will only agree to that if it is sold under the conditions and under the price formula that is found in here," which is that they will sell it under the value of a leasehold-free, simple estate.

Branch: Fair market value, not considering the leasehold that is encumbering the property.

Gattis: Right.

Branch: And then a 10 percent discount. The 10 percent discount is there because you are not considering the encumbered lease. And you are also taking into consideration all the investments that these landholders have put in, in terms of roads, improvements, and water facilities, etc. So that was the compromise.

Gattis: So the compromise is an unencumbered, fee simple estate that is a fair market value of that, unencumbered.

Branch: Without improvements, right.

Gattis: Less 10 percent. And that 10 percent is to take into consideration the fact that some of these leases have flipped multiple times.

People have paid in excess of what the actual lease value is from BRA. The fact that they have improved some of these lands, the fact that they have roads in and out of there as well, and that 10 percent discount is meant to reflect those types of investments, and that is the agreement.

Branch: Right. And hopefully this will ward off litigation and the mess that's been created out there by really unintended consequences of having thirty-year leases. And now people putting dwellings on these that have value in excess of that. And now we're in a situation where you can't attract serious capital investment because you have thirty-year leases.

Gattis: The whole intent of this bill is to avoid litigation, that this is the agreement. This is the law under which we are going to sell these. This is the equation under which we will sell them. Everybody is in agreement to that. So this should avoid litigation on this matter.

Branch: Exactly right. And it will also help those communities draw capital and economic development to that region of Texas. It is also to help people in your community by putting more cash, a huge infusion of cash, into the Brazos River, which will allow for more water development throughout Texas, which is what this bill is about.[127]

Given that Representative Dan Gattis only had six days left in his legislative career, I find it noble that he went to the trouble to document the fact that Estes' land-grab had not passed the smell test in the House Natural Resources Committee.[128] I also find it telling that he mentioned the 10 percent discount five times in the course of five minutes.

---

127 Rep. Dan Gattis, "House Session," Texas House of Representatives Broadcast Archives, 6:40:20, Texas House of Representatives, May 22, 2007, accessed July 29, 2013. rtsp:// realvideoe.house.state.tx.us:554/archives/hc80/052207a.rm.

128 Representative Dan Gattis retired after the Eightieth Legislative Session. We lost a good one there.

Following that, Representative Mike O'Day, who had also grilled Robert Aldrich during the House Natural Resources Committee hearing, asked Representative Dan Branch to yield the floor. He also asked that his conversation be reduced to writing in the House Journal for the benefit of future consideration.

> **O'Day:** Representative Branch, what happens upon the time if someone does not want to purchase their property?
>
> **Branch:** As you may know, Representative O'Day, originally the idea was that we'd continue these leases, perhaps with a new lease form. The proposal was, no, let's have people be able to buy the fee simple.
>
> There's been movement back and forth, and as I mentioned, perhaps you heard at the outset, that the amendment to the amendment, the compromise that's been worked out, will allow for transfer of property to an heir or devisee, one; two, the transfer to a lien holder.
>
> So if you have a foreclosure by a financial institution or a bankruptcy, etc., they don't have to buy the land. They can just take possession of the leasehold interest. And that the section doesn't take effect until 2011.
>
> **O'Day:** In this arrangement, didn't they clear to the purchasers or in the agreement that the BRA is going to raise leases on what's currently there if they do not purchase the land?
>
> **Branch:** That's my understanding, yes. That was one of the reasons the whole issue came about, and it was not only the lease rate but also the form of the lease.
>
> **O'Day:** Is there any force for the current lessees to have to sell the property or to purchase the property? Is there a requirement for any of the lessees to have to purchase the property?
>
> **Branch:** Not to my knowledge.
>
> **O'Day:** Okay, I didn't think so either.[129]

---

129 Rep. Mike O'Day, "House Session," Texas House of Representatives Broadcast Archives, 6:45:33, Texas House of Representatives, May 22, 2007, accessed July 30, 2013. rtsp:// realvideoe.house.state.tx.us:554/archives/hc80/052207a.rm

As there were no other questions, and the amendment was acceptable to the author of the bill, Senate Bill 1326 was adopted as Amendment 63 to the House version of Senate Bill 3. It appeared that the Hail Mary had worked one more time, and the leaseholders had won the ability to purchase the land beneath their lakefront homes, with a 10 percent discount.

Unfortunately, the Senate version of Senate Bill 3 contained no such amendment, and the discrepancy would have to be worked out in a conference committee. During that process, Amendment 63 was summarily rejected at the direction of Senator Kip Averitt.

On Sunday, May 27, 2007, the Conference Committee report on Senate Bill 3 came up for a vote on the floor of the Senate. There were twenty-nine yeas and one nay. The single no vote was cast by Senator Craig Estes. He was fur-flying furious. What happened just before the vote was cast was priceless.

Senator Chris Harris from Arlington, the hometown of the River Card, asked Lt. Governor David Dewhurst for the floor. In front of God and everyone in attendance, Harris took Averitt to the woodshed. If this were a movie instead of a case study, that exchange would be the opening scene. It is pure YouTube gold.[130] You have to treat yourself to a viewing of this video. You also have to give Senator Averitt credit for being able to graciously take a public ass-chewing with the best of them. So as not to spoil your viewing, I am not going to reduce that conversation to writing, other than to say that Senator Harris led off with, "Senator Averitt, whatever happened to a deal is a deal?"

Instead, let me offer the exchange that followed between Senator Estes and Senator Averitt. Senator Estes asked that the conversation be reduced to writing in the Senate Journal, so I will oblige him here as well.

Sunday, May 27, 2007 SENATE JOURNAL 5209—Regular Session 69th Day

REMARKS ORDERED PRINTED

On motion of Senator Estes and by unanimous consent, the exchange between Senators Averitt and Estes regarding SB 3 was

---

130 Sen. Chris Harris, "Senate Session," Senate RealMedia Video Archives, 3:16:40, Texas Senate, May 27, 2007, accessed July 30, 2013. rtsp://realvideoe.senate.state.tx.us:554/archives/2007/MAY/052707.session.rm.

ordered reduced to writing and printed in the Senate Journal as follows:

Estes: Senator Averitt, are you familiar with my work this session on a local bill very important to my constituents and the constituents of several other members in this body, which would allow residential leaseholders at Possum Kingdom Lake to buy the land under their homes from the Brazos River Authority?

Averitt: That's correct.

Estes: And do you recall that my work on this issue was manifest in the form of Senate Bill 1326, which earlier passed the Senate by a large majority and has passed the House by a large majority in the form of a floor amendment to your Senate Bill 3?

Averitt: That is correct. And let me back up on the answer to that first question.

Estes: We can take all the time you need on it.

Averitt: I know it does primarily affect the Possum Kingdom region, which is in your district, but the Brazos River Authority's jurisdiction stretches across many senatorial districts in a broad stretch of the state of Texas.

Estes: That's correct. Okay, thank you. Can you explain why the language of my bill that passed both houses by such large margins is so conspicuous by its absence from Senate Bill 3?

Averitt: Senator Estes, I know you worked very hard on that bill. And I also know that you know that I was never comfortable with how the language was written as it came out of the Senate or out of the Committee. But it was a bill with your name on it. You were moving the process forward, and I was glad to facilitate that process.

However, when it was put on as an amendment to a bill that has my name on it, I couldn't get comfortable with a piece of legislation that was gaining an automatic discount to folks, an arbitrary number discount of state property. And, therefore, I thought it best and asked the House sponsor that we take it out.

Estes: But obviously a large percentage of the body and the other body was comfortable with it, but you weren't comfortable with it.

Averitt: I was not. And there was another problem. That bill got filed at 11:59, Senator. One more amendment probably would've pushed it over the limit. So we were pushing the limit as it was.

Estes: All right. Well I appreciate you expediting it. Now your district includes McLennan County and the city of Waco, where the Brazos River Authority has its headquarters.

Averitt: McLennan County. That's correct.

Estes: Do you consider the Brazos River Authority to be a constituent of yours?

Averitt: There are several people who work at the Brazos River Authority that live in my senatorial district. There are many that work in your senatorial district, Senator Duncan's district, Senator Ogden's district, Senator Jackson's district, and on and on.

Estes: Would you agree that the Brazos River Authority is, for all practical purposes, a state agency whose primary mission is the management and conservation of its water resources?

Averitt: It is a quasi-state agency whose primary function is to maintain and preserve the resources related to the Brazos River Basin.

Estes: Can you explain how the Brazos River Authority generates the funds it needs to accomplish its mission?

Averitt: Primarily through fees they charge for the water that they manage.

Estes: Okay. So there's no general appropriations to the Brazos River Authority?

Averitt: There is none.

Estes: Okay. So even though the Brazos River Authority does not receive any general appropriations, would you agree that the money it generates to sustain its mission are, in fact, public funds and belong to the people of Texas?

Averitt: I think you're probably right on that.

Estes: Okay. Do you think a state agency like the Brazos River Authority should be allowed to use public funds to hire a lobby firm to advance and protect its interests in the Texas legislature?

Averitt: You know, that's a question that we always deal with, Senator Estes, on which group should lobby. Should teachers be allowed to lobby? Should public employees be allowed to lobby? River authorities? And so on and so forth. It's an issue that is debated in this chamber time and again.

Estes: What do you think?

Averitt: I think there are, certainly, instances where that's a necessary function.

Estes: So, in other words, this money that belongs to the people of Texas is being used to hire powerful lobby firms in Austin to thwart the will of this Senate and this House?

Averitt: I'm not aware of their using lobby money to thwart the will of the Senate. I'm not advised on any of that.

Estes: Do you think the Texas legislature exercises sufficient oversight of the Brazos River Authority and other river authorities?

Averitt: That's another question of, you know, that will be debated as we go forward. There was an extensive study done a few years ago on whether or not a river authority should undergo sunset.

Estes: Well, that was my next question.

Averitt: And it was determined at that time, that that was probably not an appropriate course of action. Senator Estes, I know that that's an issue that's on your mind, it's on Senator Hegar's mind, and it should be an item of discussion as we go forward.

Estes: Well, I was just asking what you think about it. Do you think these river authorities, including the Brazos River Authority, should be, perhaps go through the sunset process?

Averitt: I look forward to studying that issue with you.

Estes: All right. So you're undecided? Okay. In the future would you be willing to work with me, our colleagues, and perhaps the governor's office on the concerns some of us have with management and operations of the Brazos River Authority and other river authorities?

Averitt: We should always be concerned with the management of any of the, of our public or quasi-public agencies.

Estes: All right. I'm just about finished here. Chairman Averitt, I appreciate you for having this conversation with me publicly, and I appreciate the opportunity to serve as your vice-chairman of the Senate Natural Resources Committee. I am looking forward to working with you on these and other issues in the days ahead. I thank you.[131]

---

131 "Senate Journal," Eightieth Legislature—Regular Session, Texas Senate, May 27, 2007, p. 5209, accessed July 30, 2013. http://www.journals.senate.state.tx.us/sjrnl/80r/html/80RSJ05-27-F.HTM.

This conversation ended the legislative efforts to force the Brazos River Authority to sell the shoreline of Possum Kingdom Lake in 2007. To set the stage for the future, Senator Estes publicly threatened to eliminate the Brazos River Authority altogether, if that was what it took to get what he wanted.

Doing so would prove to be unnecessary. As was mentioned earlier, Governor Perry's director of appointments, Mr. Ken Anderson, was monitoring the divestiture process and evaluating the performance of his appointees. A great many of these had failed their respective IQ tests and demonstrated that they were incapable of reading an org-chart. This would provide yet another opportunity for Governor Perry to put his reputation as a governor who "transparently rewards friends and punishes enemies" to good use.[132]

Similarly, Lt. Governor David Dewhurst would be called upon to complement the governor's efforts by wielding both his overt and covert powers over the Texas Senate. While Governor Perry would be required to neutralize the opposition on the board of the BRA, Lt. Governor Dewhurst would be required to eliminate the opposition within the Senate. And because the "three amigos" prefer to work in unison, Attorney General Greg Abbott would be required to neutralize the laws that were designed to prevent a deal of this nature from occurring and contributed to the failure of Senate Bill 1326.

---

132 "Rick Perry is 2010 Texan of the Year," *Dallas Morning News*, December 26, 2010, accessed March 1, 2013. http://www.dallasnews.com/opinion/sunday-commentary/20101226-editorial-rick-perry-is-the-2010-texan-of-the-year.ece

Intermission

To be sure, the directors of the Brazos River Authority had waged and won a major battle during the Eightieth Legislative Session of 2007. In the face of extreme political pressure, these directors individually and collectively fulfilled the oath that they had made to the taxpayers of Texas.

> I, *Appointed Official,* do solemnly swear (or affirm), that I will faithfully execute the duties of the office of Board Director of the Brazos River Authority of the State of Texas, and will to the best of my ability preserve, protect, and defend the Constitution and laws of the United States and of this State, so help me God.[133]

Of course, that was the problem. The BRA board directors were actually trying to uphold their respective oaths. And that was a problem that would have to be resolved by the governor and his staff.

For those of you who have been scoring along at home, you are no doubt aware that the first half of 2007 was spent arguing over whether to sell the lakefront property at Possum Kingdom Lake for $200 million, or $180 million, or maybe even $95 million. And all the while, I have been

---

133 The Texas Constitution, Article 16. General Provisions, Sec. 1. (a). http://www.statutes. legis.state.tx.us/Docs/CN/htm/CN.16.htm

asserting that the property that was sold for $50 million was actually worth $1 billion.

So whose analysis is wrong here?

Compare these price tags to the lakefront property that Governor Rick Perry sold on March 30, 2007, during this same period of time. That sale equated to $2.3 million per acre. For future reference, you should also consider the following sequence of events chronicled by the *Dallas News*.[134]

June 12, 2000: Norman Hurd sells his ten-acre family estate on Lake LBJ, renamed the Peninsula, to Horseshoe Bay Resort Inc., owned by Doug Jaffe.

Sept. 19, 2000: Senator Troy Fraser (R-Horseshoe Bay) buys two newly subdivided Peninsula lots from Horseshoe Bay Resort for $1 million.

Feb. 28, 2001: Governor Perry purchases a half-acre Peninsula lot from Troy Fraser, a longtime childhood friend, for $300,000, plus $10,762 in interest.

Nov. 30, 2001: Governor Perry, through Attorney Colleen McHugh, chairwoman of the Texas Public Safety Commission, appeals the tax appraisal on his Peninsula lot. Colleen McHugh does not charge a fee.

Dec. 14, 2001: Stan Hemphill, chief appraiser for the Burnet County Appraisal District, agrees to lower the assessment on Perry's Peninsula lot from $414,700 to $310,762. This is the exact same amount as Governor Perry's purchase price.

May 2005: After talking with Ron Mitchell, the resort vice chairman, Perry lists his Peninsula lot for sale with Horseshoe

---

134 James Drew, Steve McGonigle, and Ryan McNeill, "Murkey Land Deals Mark Gov. Rick Perry's Past," *Dallas News*, July 25, 2010, accessed March 1, 2011. http://www.dallasnews. com/news/politics/state-politics/20100725-murky-land-deals-mark-gov.-rick-perry_s-past.ece.

Bay Resort Realty for about $1.2 million. He pulls the listing after about five months without receiving any offers.

Oct. 11, 2005: Governor Perry appoints Colleen McHugh to the University of Texas System Board of Regents.

Jan. 1, 2007: The Burnet County Appraisal District raises the appraisal on Perry's Peninsula lot to $600,000.

March 30, 2007: Responding to an offer conveyed through Ron Mitchell, Perry sells his lot to Alan Moffatt for $1.15 million. Horseshoe Bay Resort Realty does not charge a commission.

Feb. 9, 2009: Governor Perry appoints Ron Mitchell to the Texas State University System Board of Regents.

An appraiser hired by the *Dallas News* determined that the lake lot that Governor Perry purchased was actually worth $450,000 when he bought it. That same appraiser, who had decades of experience in Horseshoe Bay real estate, also determined that Governor Perry's sale price was $350,000 above market value.

With this transaction, Governor Perry laid out a precise game plan for how the leaseholders at Possum Kingdom should parlay their lakefront investments. Step 1 is to take possession. Step 2 is to manipulate the assessed value. Step 3 is to manipulate the sales price. With the help of the governor and many others, they would do so.

In less than seven years, Governor Perry had almost tripled his money on that lakefront property, earning a profit of over $800,000. In my humble opinion, that is some pretty savvy investing. It does make me wonder, though, how Governor Perry could possible say no to a wealthy contingency when he had just completed a whorehouse lakefront deal of his own. The answer is that he really couldn't and that he really needed this topic to go away. The same can be said for Lt. Governor David Dewhurst. The last thing that either of these two needed was for someone to start examining people's real estate deals.

Terry Sullivan, the campaign manager for Kay Bailey Hutchison in 2009, characterized Rick Perry's investment prowess somewhat differently in an article written by noted political columnist Jay Root.

> Rick Perry should do an infomercial on how to become a millionaire as a professional politician. From abusing his power over appointments to getting sweetheart real estate deals from supporters, he's a regular get-rich-quick icon.[135]

Governor Perry's aides countered in the same article that the governor "has benefited from nothing more than strong business acumen and good timing." Jay Root offered two such examples of that good timing.

> Perry once sold a 9.3-acre tract to computer magnate Michael Dell for nearly four times what he paid for it, using influential Texas lobbyist Mike Toomey as the broker. The West Austin property sold for $465,000 in 1995 and gave the Dell estate badly needed access to an adjacent municipal sewage district.
>
> A little more than a year later, Perry snapped up 60 acres southwest of Austin, after acting on a tip from flamboyant developer Gary Bradley, whose real estate empire fell into bankruptcy in 2002. The property was sold two and a half years later at a $239,000 profit. Perry has also bought and sold houses and raw land for various gains since he won statewide office in 1990.

Like I said, welcome to the great state of Texas where we are "Wide Open for Business."

Large poker tournaments use scheduled intermissions to give the players a break from the action. The first intermission also provides an opportunity to color up, rebuy, and add-on.

Coloring up is an exercise of exchanging a large number of poker chips for a smaller number of chips of a higher denomination while keeping the total value of the chipstack the same. A rebuy is the purchase of a number of chips equal to the original buy-in. An add-on is the purchase of additional chips over and above the buy-in and any rebuys.

---

135 Jay Root, "Gov. Rick Perry's Wealth Fueled by Buying and Selling Texas Land," *Lubbock Avalanche-Journal*, September 27, 2007, accessed March 1, 2013. http://lubbockonline.com/stories/092709/sta_497947023.shtml.

The River Card claimed in his thank-you note entitled *Unsung Heroes* that he was watching from the sidelines during 2007. In poker, we call this the rail. While it might be true that the River Card was standing behind the rail, it is also possible that he was simply playing tight.

In calendar year 2007, the River Card's political contributions totaled $3,350. Over the next thirty-six months, his political contributions totaled $82,500 and went to the key politicians involved in this deal. By no means am I suggesting that the River Card was coloring up, or rebuying, or buying an add-on. But I also cannot help but notice that his political contributions in 2011 and 2012, after his deal was done, totaled a mere $2,000.

During Round I, the leaseholders and their political allies snatched defeat from the jaws of victory. During Round II, the River Card would show everyone involved how the game is really played.

Cheers.